Prai

Beyond Equality is a thought-provoking exploration of agency, identity, and empowerment in the lives of women leaders. Through philosophical ponderings, personal narratives, and sociological analysis, this book delves into the profound significance of agency in shaping the trajectories of women's lives. Advancing a concept of responsive agency, Landerholm makes a compelling argument that women need to set their sights far beyond equality to a whole new realm. This book serves as a rallying cry for women to reclaim their narratives, redefine success on their own terms, and catalyze meaningful change in their communities and institutions. In Landerholm's world, women find agency not in spite of, but because of, the barriers and constraints they encounter.

—Dianna Shandy, provost and vice president of academic affairs, Augustana College, and coauthor of *Glass Ceilings and 100-Hour Couples: What the Opt-Out Phenomenon Can Teach Us about Work and Family*

A fresh look at the gendered realities of institutions, *Beyond Equality* illuminates the lives and careers of the exceptional women of higher education. Empirically grounded and accessibly written, the book will be a helpful addition to conversations among both scholars and practitioners.

—Lisa Weaver Swartz, sociologist and author of *Stained Glass Ceilings: How Evangelicals Do Gender and Practice Power*

Landerholm's book uses the term "insanity" in a way that makes me feel sane. So often as a woman who is a leader in educational administration and Christian ministry, I find maddening the ways in which both sorts of institutions minimize the differing experiences of female- and male-bodied persons. Even worse, I find that pointing out obvious differences causes me and other women to be less trusted and less professionally marketable. Landerholm presents what I would consider a realistic interpretation of what is difficult about the man's world that the academy remains. She also provides hope that, when we get past competitive mindsets, we might be able to work across differences to improve higher education as a whole.

—Sarah B. Drummond, founding dean, Andover Newton Seminary at Yale Divinity School

Beyond Equality offers useful blueprints for any woman seeking to reshape the landscape of leadership so top jobs can offer the kind of power women really need: the power to redefine success on their own terms.

—Marcia Alesan Dawkins, senior research scientist, Center for Creative Leadership

BEYOND EQUALITY

BEYOND EQUALITY

Women Leaders in Higher Education

Savanah N. Landerholm

FORTRESS PRESS
Minneapolis

BEYOND EQUALITY
Women Leaders in Higher Education

Copyright © 2024 Fortress Press, an imprint of 1517 Media. All rights reserved. Except for brief quotations in critical articles or reviews, no part of this book may be reproduced in any manner without prior written permission from the publisher. Email copyright@1517.media or write to Permissions, Fortress Press, PO Box 1209, Minneapolis, MN 55440-1209.

29 28 27 26 25 24   1 2 3 4 5 6 7 8 9

Library of Congress Cataloging-in-Publication Data

Names: Landerholm, Savanah N., author.
Title: Beyond equality : women leaders in higher education / Savanah N. Landerholm.
Description: Minneapolis : Fortress Press, [2024] | Includes bibliographical references and index.
Identifiers: LCCN 2024019041 (print) | LCCN 2024019042 (ebook) | ISBN 9798889831754 (paperback) | ISBN 9798889831761 (ebook)
Subjects: LCSH: Leadership in women. | Women in higher education. | Feminism and higher education.
Classification: LCC HD6054.3 .L36 2024 (print) | LCC HD6054.3 (ebook) | DDC 658.4/09082--dc23/eng/20240709
LC record available at https://lccn.loc.gov/2024019041
LC ebook record available at https://lccn.loc.gov/2024019042

Cover design: Kristin Miller

Print ISBN: 979-8-8898-3175-4
eBook ISBN: 979-8-8898-3176-1

To my three little ladies,
may you always be brave.

CONTENTS

	Acknowledgments	ix
	Preface	xiii
1.	The Insanity of Equality	1
2.	Passers *How Fitting In Is Not Enough*	19
3.	Pushers *How Sheer Determination Is Not Enough*	35
4.	Peacekeepers *How Playing by the Rules Is Not Enough*	49
5.	Beyond Equality *The Ethics of Responsive Agency*	69
	Appendix 1: Rubric for Classifying Institutions	91
	Appendix 2: Participant Information	93
	Appendix 3: Researcher Positionality Statement	95
	Notes	97
	Bibliography	123
	Index	133

ACKNOWLEDGMENTS

As I near the end of this longer-than-expected process, I realize my reliance on the strength of community to make this book a physical reality.

My hard-working husband, Scott, kept me laughing and kept me going. There is no way to name all of the countless ways that he contributed to my completion. From domestic life to moral support, Scott instilled confidence where I lacked it. Scott celebrated my accomplishments from finishing semesters to finishing coursework to passing comps. We married young and have grown up together—that doesn't come without challenges—but it has been quite a series of adventures! Through ups and downs, Scott has believed in me and stood with me. I am forever grateful for his determination in his own work as he waited and worked with me to finish.

My three darling daughters, to whom this book is dedicated, served as my motivation to write and keep writing. Thank you for your patience, your giggles, and your love—Ivy, Selah, and Noelle.

My dear dad, Dr. Tom Nisbett, is my editor-for-life and my constant encourager. He made the long drive to Texas countless times to rock a baby so I could work, to quiz me as I prepared for comps in graduate school, and to process with me as I wrote this book. My dad spoke truth when my head filled with doubts, and he kept me on course when I lost track of true North. His peace and confidence in me helped me tackle each hurdle. He often says I did not need him, but I certainly would not have wanted to make this journey without his companionship. My dad has always been a model of how I want to treat others. His very presence increases my level of hope as he radiates Christ's love and deep care.

My mom, Lou Ann Nisbett, modeled what it can look like to love your work and love your family well. She is a type-A personality who taught me how to get things done and to start at four o'clock in the morning. I've watched my mom excel and overachieve in her work, and she inspired me to do the same. She taught me how to "do my homework" on everything from home remodeling to car buying. My mom operates out of a growth mindset, believing that she can learn the ropes with time, sweat, and dedication.

My in-laws, Rev. Kurt and Nancy Landerholm, supported us in practical ways that made life more manageable. I am grateful for their regular visits when they cared for my daughters, stocked up our freezer and our cabinets, and cleaned our house from top to bottom. The royal treatment they lavished on us was above and beyond what we could have asked for or imagined. My in-laws have taught me a great deal about generosity, and their kindness repeatedly encouraged me and fueled me forward.

Drs. Carey and Leanne Newman have supported me far beyond what anyone will ever understand. Sandwiched between Carey, first my boss and later my editor, and Leanne, whom I became acquainted with as a professor in my department, I felt like I was practically part of the Newman family. Carey is my sponsor: he planted the seed for me to start a doctoral program and advocated for me every step of the way through the completion of this book. He often reminded me that he got me into this program, and he would help me through it. True to his promise, Carey challenged and empowered me professionally while he championed me academically. I am and will forever be indebted to Carey for his generous investment in me as an employee, a scholar, a leader, and an author. In times when I thought I should slow my pace or felt overwhelmed by the different route I was taking, Leanne put my perspective in check and helped me chart a realistic and achievable path to a "done" dissertation. Leanne reminded me of the value of enjoying my family while pursuing my goals.

Thank you to Dr. Nathan Alleman, who guided me in my initial research. You helped me navigate the path from student to scholar.

Acknowledgments

A special thanks to two providential friends, whose friendships refreshed me as I wrapped up my writing. First, my gratitude to Dr. Donald K. McKim for his faithful support, wonderful wisdom, and persistent prayer on my behalf. I feel honored to call him friend and humbled that he accompanied me on this journey. Second, my heartfelt thanks to Susan Cooper for taking interest in my work and for praying consistently for me.

Finally, to all of my friends and colleagues near and far, who were understanding with my research, study, writing, and re-writing, I am so grateful to have cultivated special relationships even in the midst of a very busy and demanding season. Specifically, I want to thank my sweet sisters, my dear covenant group, my goals group, and my church life group, who kept me motivated and encouraged throughout the long writing journey. These admirable women kept me accountable, brought my family dinners, taught me how to be an intentional mother, and cheered me on to the finish line.

PREFACE

MOMENTS SPENT CARING for a newborn remind me of the uniqueness of a woman. From the physical pressures of labor, delivery, and nursing, to the emotional overload of acquainting herself with this new person, a woman experiences the birth and care of a baby differently than a man. Although I have spent much of my life, and even my education, advocating for the equality of women, having a baby forces me to acknowledge that while women deserve equal respect and equal opportunities, the needs of women and men are indeed different.[1] And, although many differences in the workplace are not affiliated with gender, I do find gender to be a reminder that needs, approaches, and styles vary. Of course, personal experience is the refrain of life. My research stems from my own life experiences as a woman who felt misunderstood and, in moments, devalued for having a baby in graduate school. Out of my desire for future women to have a better experience, I sought to reveal the experiences of women leaders who persevered.

My love of learning linked with love for my family fueled my research, my writing, my advocacy for women, and my pursuit of balance. I have immersed myself in all there is to read on women and leadership and work-life balance. At some point, I began to question if this was old news. I know problems persist for women, but there has been a lot of progress. I am a glass-half-full person, and with notable improvement for women, I want to rejoice. I think we ought to celebrate the increased awareness, the changes in parental leave policies, and especially the women who have succeeded. Even so, more women are inhibited by barriers than are able to overcome them.[2] While there has been progress, inequalities persist. In short, the problem still exists; it is yesterday's news *and* today's news but hopefully not tomorrow's news.

For decades (if not millennia), women participated in the workplace without leading it. Certainly, women had an increase in access to traditionally male-dominated jobs, but this was not equivalent to an increase in access to high-quality or high-ranking positions of leadership.[3] Moreover, while the role of the woman was shifting, gender roles for men had not been similarly reconsidered.[4] In effect, men were not entering the private sphere of housework in comparable numbers.[5] Men had been known as the leader (not to be confused with the manager) of the house and the provider for their families. A good man was believed to "act with aggressiveness, dominance, and courage."[6] Society assigned women the more delicate and instable qualities, which did not deem women as fit for leadership.[7] Thus, men took the lead—after all, this *was* their traditional role. However, traditional roles were under scrutiny, and women began to call these normative assignments into question.

Being a woman in this unprecedented time in history is complex. Women are the domestic caretakers: mothers, housewives, homeschool teachers. Women are working professionals: empowered, in charge, managers, leaders. Not all of these identities are worn by every woman, yet these spheres overlap. As I began writing this in the midst of the coronavirus pandemic, I worked from home with my whole family at home. My experience mirrors that of many other women who are working from home with "coworkers" who require help in the bathroom, help with schoolwork, help to reach snacks and toys. Early data is showing that with the closure of schools and childcare, women, even working-from-home women, are taking the primary role as teacher and nanny.[8] Although men are also working from home, they are more often operating with a protected workday at home. The news is reporting on this, but anecdotally, this is the struggle many women face. Work has been relegated to early mornings, late nights, and nap times. Equality for women seems to be even further away. Meanwhile, pressures continue to pile up with no relief in sight.

The role of women in domestic and workforce spheres has changed significantly over the last century, but it would be a mistake to conclude that a new day has dawned for women in the workforce and for women in higher education in particular. Developing woman-friendly legal, corporate, and educational contexts do not generate women leaders.[9] Let me say that again, *promoting equity legally, corporately, and educationally does not produce women leaders*. Not only do gender discrimination and barriers still exist, but also the presence of a large number of women in the academic pipeline does not necessarily lead to women in leadership in higher education or in society at large. In fact, the dearth of women leaders in higher education is illustrative of the problem for women in all spheres. Self-reflective and slow-moving, higher education offers a window through which we can examine the basic premise of the problem for all women: all women have to make impossible choices.

I wondered if this book was still relevant, but I wonder no more. Clearly, we still need to talk about this. Women need to learn from the experiences of female leaders who have gone before them, and they need permission to navigate their own situation with confidence and courage in their own way. There are no easy solutions if there are indeed any solutions at all. This book is for women launching their career—trying to climb the professional ladder but facing holdups. This book is for women who find themselves working with children—pressed between progressing at work and being present with their families. This book is for women who have persevered and desire comradery—other women who can relate to their journey. Rich with experiences of women pioneers, this book sheds insight on the past while seeking a way forward—toward *and* beyond equality—for all working women.

CHAPTER ONE

The Insanity of Equality

IN THE BEGINNING, *men*.[1] Men are the main characters throughout world history. Men made history and men wrote history. These two are not unrelated. Male supremacy determined religious and cultural norms from surnames to inheritance to gender roles. The unspoken—or at times, crudely spoken—belief that women are less than men not only saturated western culture, but it determined the roles women could play in business and higher education. The girls-versus-boys debates start as far back as the playground, but sentiments of this long-standing dispute follow women well into the workplace. American culture socializes girls from a young age that women are weak and fragile. Men are depicted as surpassing women in brute strength, emotional strength, and mental capacity,[2] whereas women are considered *lesser*. Women are considered less powerful—less strength, less endurance, less force. Women are considered less qualified—less educated, less knowledgeable, less experienced. Women are considered less capable—less dominating, less aggressive, less decisive. Though these are *just* stereotypes, the message is crystal clear that women are less than men.

The disjunction of men and women meant men enjoyed privileges not granted to women. Men accessed formal education as well as worked and led in the marketplace.[3] A *good* man was educated and contributed to society through his work. A *good* woman married, produced offspring, and managed the work of the home.[4] Culture established this way of life as normal, and religious views upheld this as the system of order.[5] Undeniably, marriage and motherhood are wonderfully important roles and extremely valuable to society. Raising good citizens and kind human beings is an enormous task worthy of great honor and respect. Nevertheless, for most of human history, women were relegated to second-class citizenship, treated as less valuable than men, and inhibited from engaging in all spheres of society.

Females stayed separate from and unequal to men for hundreds of years, but women increasingly chafed against being solely occupied with domestic concerns and not qualified to engage in any other sphere.[6] Women sought entrance into higher education alongside appeals for voting rights. Colleges and universities gradually permitted coeducation, allowing men and women to study at the same institution, but the course work and expectations typically differed. Courses for women focused on reinforcing traditional gender roles by preparing women for a particular set of "helping" careers (homemaking, educating, nursing).[7] In other words, women accessed education without accessing the *same* education as men, but it marked an expansion of a woman's place beyond the home—progress. Access to higher education increased for both men and women after the Second World War, and college continued to gain importance as a prerequisite to a successful life.[8] The percentage of women in college increased significantly in the 1960s—representing a swelling consciousness of gender equity. In the early 1990s, women became as likely as men to earn a bachelor's degree, but women steadily began to exceed men in college completion rates.[9] The upward trend continued, and now, the percentage of women college students hits new highs. Women outnumber men as college graduates—earning about 60 percent of bachelor's degrees and nearly 60 percent of all master's degrees. Now, women even earn more doctorates than men (just over 53 percent).[10] With equal access to education at all levels, women are just as qualified as men for work—statistics suggest there are numerically *more* qualified women. Even so, participation in the workforce required overcoming additional barriers for women.

Easily one of the most notable social and economic changes in the last century has been the influx of educated women into the workforce.[11] Women represent about half of the US population (50.8 percent), but traditionally, they have not held parallel representation to men in the labor force.[12] Interestingly, the realities of war in the first half of the twentieth century required women's participation in the workforce when men were absent. The wartime circumstances gave women permission to assume multiple roles, yet when the war ended, a woman's ability to have a career *and* a family became uncertain once again.[13] Many women chose to stay in the labor force and accessed higher-level jobs (previously only available to men). The labor force participation of married women with young children increased more than fivefold in just sixty years.[14] The accumulative entry of women completely transformed the landscape of the labor force as well as the role of the American woman.

The working woman challenged the traditional role of a woman and produced widespread cultural impact. Working women today benefit from educational opportunities women in their mother's generation never had. Some women work simply because they find their jobs gratifying, but many more women juggle work and children because their families depend on them.[15] No matter the reason, more women (more educated women in particular) enter and work in the labor force than ever before in history—making the goal of equality seem within reach.

Equality matters for preparation as well as performance. Women first needed equal *access* to education in order to be considered in the workplace. Now, equality is measured by participation, by compensation, by acceptance, by title, and by power. Equality in any one of these areas would be considered remarkable progress because women lag men on all of these indicators.[16] The cultural narrative suggests that these measures are indelibly linked, yet equal numbers of men and women do not yield equal pay or equal power for men and women.

As women sought equality with men in the workplace, women faced barriers. Despite progress, women were not initially as qualified—as educated, as equipped, or as experienced—as most men. Women found their way into traditionally male-dominated jobs but lacked experience and mentorship, which blocked them from high-quality or high-ranking positions of leadership. When women began their careers, the glass ceiling was undetectable and irrelevant, but, later, this invisible barrier would keep them from attaining equal leadership authority with men. Glass ceilings kept women from climbing up the corporate ladder by blocking and preventing their progress. The women who broke through the glass ceilings at their institutions—becoming the first woman to hold their position—deserve to have their stories narrated. These women did not always face a warm reception: "Some of these firsts meant I was facing obstacles, because people would question if I was trying to usurp someone else's position, a man's, or if I was really claiming a rightful place."[17] The women who have been successful are viewed as the exceptions—the lucky or fortunate—rather than as capable and the clear choice for the position.

On the other end of the ladder, some women found themselves in sticky-floor jobs, which are jobs essential to the functioning of the organization but often viewed as insignificant. The metaphor became widely known after research that measured male and female health professionals who began their careers at the same time.[18] Women would get stuck in a low-level job, with low pay and low rank, unable to advance into a higher-level job. Women not only stayed in these jobs in reality but also in culture's collective imagination. A secretary, a receptionist, an assistant—a woman. Women, more so than men, who enter low-level jobs have limited opportunity for advancement primarily due to the lack of nurture (mentorship or personal investment).

While glass ceilings and sticky floors could affect any woman, women with children experienced a distinctive barrier. The barrier commonly called maternal walls are unwritten expectations for women to exit the workplace once they have children. Unfortunately, maternal status changes the way a woman is viewed and treated in the workplace. Women, if not pushed out during pregnancy, are "mommy tracked" or blocked from upward mobility in the organization after having children.[19] Despite the legal efforts to eliminate discrimination against mothers in the workplace, maternal walls have not completely come down.[20] As one woman put it: "Universities can have their policies, but the way that people behave is the way the people behave. You can't legislate that."[21] In other words, culture does not always mirror structural changes.

Even so, more women have become senior leaders, and the concepts of the glass ceiling, the sticky floor, and the maternal wall are no longer impenetrable barriers. Glass has been broken, floors have been cleaned, and walls have (legislative and operational) ladders. The glass ceiling has cracked, and in some cases dramatically so. Women now head some of the world's most powerful and successful companies—General Motors, Best Buy, Northrop Grumman, Gap, Advanced Micro Devices, and United Parcel Services all have female CEOs.[22] Though women senior leaders are not yet the norm in Fortune 500 companies, women have been making strides. As of 2023, about 10 percent of the biggest American companies were run by women—the highest percentage in the history of the Fortune 500, yet far from equal.[23] But, the presence of women leaders shows women have made progress in the workforce.

Progress for women is evidenced through participation in education, in the labor force, and in leadership, though inequality persists, particularly at leadership levels. Originally this incongruity was explained as a pipeline problem: the belief that there were not enough women eligible for leadership positions.[24] The pipeline metaphor assumed that the number of women inputted into the system (attending college, graduate school) would be equal to the number of women at the top of the system (CEOs, presidents). However, with current equality of access to education and access to work, the pipeline is full of educated, capable, experienced women, but men still hold the majority of leadership positions.[25] Despite a rapid surge of qualified and motivated women into the workforce, policies and structures in businesses and organizations have not kept up with the adjustments necessary for their new population of employees. Perhaps an unidentified clog or a leak in the pipeline may keep women from rising to senior leadership, or perhaps women simply face structural constraints.[26] The problem with the pipeline, then, is that the presence of a large pool of educated, working women does not inevitably lead to women in leadership. Or, perhaps *equality of education, experience, and access is simply not enough.*

The historical and cultural component of being considered less or not enough gets stuck in the female psyche. For some women, this inhibits progress, while for others it fuels their pursuit to prove themselves. Modern culture's response to gender inequity has been to demonstrate that women are not weak, untrained, or incompetent. In short, women are *not* less than men. Contemporary culture has admitted, however reluctantly, that women have what it takes. Systems morphed to make this realization a reality through equal access to education and equal access to jobs, along with dozens of cultural moves toward equality. Women were offered legal protections and *equal* opportunities: employers were required by law to consider job candidates without discriminating based on gender and working potential. Doors previously locked to women were unlocking. Fresh hope materialized for women to be equals with men in the professional sphere. The forward progress seemed promising but proved to be superficial rather than substantive. Laws changed but attitudes did not; opportunities existed but selection was low; women's roles altered but men's roles did not. Society has indeed enacted change, but women are still underpaid, overwhelmed, and downright discontent. *Either society has not yet reached the goal or the goal did not meet expectations.*

The strains of the domestic sphere combined with the stresses of the workplace produce exhausted women who are downtrodden instead of elevated. The Covid-19 pandemic's period of shelter-in-place heightened the pressure on women to perform. Women experienced, yet again, the impossibilities of work and family life.[27] Work continued but children were left without care and new solutions had to be devised; the invasion of virtual schooling battled with boundaryless remote work; loneliness or too much togetherness interfered with achieving work goals.[28] Covid-19 evidently caused a regression in the progress of women; some termed it "the gendered pandemic" for the unequal burden of unpaid care work for mothers.[29] In the wake of the global pandemic, women are searching for a sustainable way forward where they can thrive.

Necessary but Insufficient

Understanding the progress that women have made in the spheres of education, workforce, and leadership is essential to a richer understanding of the current expectations and experiences of women. Indeed, women have made massive cultural strides toward equality. Women are not less than men; a woman is equal to a man. Yet, despite significant shifts in the role of women in domestic and workforce spheres, barriers remain, particularly for women seeking to become senior leaders. It is tempting to think that championing equality and fostering a women-friendly legal, corporate, and educational context would naturally generate women leaders, but a deeper look reveals this is not the case.[30]

Society's attempts to achieve equality in the last century have produced women plagued by feeling not enough, yet working to prove that they are. Women may still feel a need to choose between work and family—a dilemma that's been around for a few decades but remains unsolved. If a woman tries to work outside the home and mother simultaneously, she feels less successful in both. Cultural forces like social media allow for constant comparison and increased feelings of failure. Ultimately, women do not pursue leadership, because based on their own assessment, they can hardly maintain the demands of their "average" lifestyle. In other words, how could she manage putting even more responsibility on her already overloaded plate? Today, women carry the first shift (work), second shift (domestic), and newly recognized third shift (health and well-being) of the family.[31] Upon reflection, it's not about a woman being equal to a man; a woman must be *more* than a man.

A woman must be more even when her tank is empty—a recognizable sensation. A woman feels like she has nothing more to give, but she finds the strength to make dinner for her children, ready them for bed, and sing them to sleep. A woman may feel she has nothing more to give, yet she works into the wee hours and completes what tomorrow demands of her. Man's story is one of pressing in, persevering, forging a way ahead. So, more political battles, more policy changes, and more personnel pressure may prove the remedy to absolute gender equality, but perhaps equality is the wrong goal. Equality appears as the promised salvation, the gold standard, the finish line. But lest women arrive at equality with expectations of freedom from their overburdened schedules, paychecks equal to male colleagues, abundant help with domestic duties, and truckloads of overdue respect, the goal ought to be reexamined.

Before equality, a woman was not afforded a seat at the table. Her voice was irrelevant and unnecessary to the conversation. As equality dawns, a woman earns a seat at the table, but women's experience shows that her seat does not guarantee her voice is heard, nor does it ensure influence or respect. The expectations and experiences of women leaders reveal that equality is not nearly enough. Current structure inherently resists and undermines women's efforts to combine work and family. While women struggle to work within the constraints of these structures, the culture further discourages women from deviating out of traditional gender norms. To move beyond equality, women need support, not judgment or hurdles. Yet, women are starved for nurture, which is the very thing that motivates and readies women to be leaders.

Perhaps achieving equality does not inherently secure value; rather, equality may be valueless: void of honor, respect, kindness, fairness, trust. Equality is the state of being equal, especially in status, rights, and opportunities. Equality is not enough in and of itself—a prerequisite but not the goal. Indeed, *it is necessary, but it is insufficient*. Equality is only part of the solution. Equality, as good as it is (and it is good), simply will not get women where they want to go. In fact, the enigma of equality is that it levels the gap between men and women, but in doing so, equality fails to allow room for differences, fails to recognize (and appreciate) the beauty of variety, and fails to place equal value on their nuances. There may be a more worthy goal after all.

Lenses of Structure, Culture, and Nurture

The stories in this book illuminate the progress of women—from work-life balance to career advancement—but they also serve as a reminder that there is not one clear path for women, although there are some explanations for why women are slow to fill senior leadership positions: *structure* (policies and practices), *culture* (internal and external pressures), and *nurture* (models and mentors). The confluence of these ideas sets the stage for a greater understanding of the barriers for women in the workplace.

Structure

The architecture of organizations ensures that women encounter more structural obstacles than men do.[32] Even when an organization espouses an ideology of meritocracy—that compensation should be defined by achievement, rather than by gender, race, religion, influence, or socioeconomic status—the enactment of these values is surprisingly slow.[33] In this sense, structure includes persistent gender discrimination and bias in organizational settings, which impede women's advancement.[34]

Initially, women faced strong resistance from men, and even other women, about their entrance into the workforce. Resistance typically came in the form of blatant bias against women. Employers did not try to hide their beliefs that women were capable of less, so women were given "lightweight" tasks and offered lower-level positions.[35] Until discriminatory acts became addressed by policy and law, public prejudice was permissible.[36] Today, resistance or overt discrimination is illegal and, as a result, less common.[37] More commonly experienced covert discrimination, also known as second-generation gender bias, is subtle and entrenched in stereotypes and organizational processes and can be hard to detect.[38] Second-generation gender bias lingers in the workplace and hinders women middle managers from becoming senior leaders.[39] Women experience less direct but more complex types of workplace inequality, which persists primarily because of a lack of awareness, not because of a desire to exclude or harm.[40]

Even so, current organizational structures are constructed based on a white male norm due to the historic dominance of whites in America. Most people agree that structural change is necessary to resolve these inherent biases,[41] however, organizational *structures* cannot change unless organizational *culture* and *nurture* practices and policies change as well. Women experience this complexity and recognize that people can be as influential as policies in establishing lasting change. Deeply rooted in culture, covert discrimination hinders women from reaching their full potential. Women struggle to excel at work and at home simultaneously and seek answers for how to negotiate both roles. Second-generation bias is difficult to pinpoint at first. However, time and again, subtle bias surfaces when women describe their experiences at work: feeling less connected with coworkers, being guided toward positions with less responsibility (and less opportunity for upward mobility) to accommodate family, or not being considered for a key position.[42] In other words, these elusive forces of discrimination are what create the sticky floors, glass ceilings, and maternal walls that keep women from progressing in the workplace.

As women seek to navigate through systemic bias, the metaphor of the labyrinth provides a perspicacious perspective. Barriers are not impassable in a labyrinth, but women must work to traverse obstacles to achieve positions of leadership.[43] The labyrinth metaphor more accurately reflects women's participation in the workforce by implying that there are numerous obstacles unique to women that they must navigate throughout their careers—not simply toward the beginning *or* the end. Experiences of systemic bias are common for women, which puts the onus for change on the system rather than the woman facing these barriers. When people become aware of the subtle and persistent effects of second-generation bias in stereotypes and organizational practices, *change is possible*.[44] Awareness does not equal change, but it opens the door to it.

Culture

Culture is a set of shared values and beliefs, and it affects what people perceive and how they behave.[45] Women's relatively new participation in all levels of the workforce challenges current organizational norms and values. Working women are worn out from juggling work and domestic responsibilities—a reality exacerbated by the Covid-19 pandemic.[46] As a result, these educated and qualified women are opting for less commitment at work in order to manage their families at home.[47] Work-life balance is not a new concept, yet women leaders are developing new coping strategies. Some women seek to excel in both work and family, deviating from societal norms, while other educated and qualified women have joined the "opt-out revolution" and stepped back from their career to attend to their family.[48]

Women, even working women, typically shoulder more of the domestic responsibilities than men. The after-hours work required at home has been labeled the second shift.[49] Among working mothers and fathers, married mothers average nearly double the housework of married fathers.[50] Disproportionate domestic responsibilities continue to be part of the discussion about gender parity in the workforce, because there is still disagreement about the optimal distribution of responsibilities for the second shift at home. Because of the increased access of women in the workplace, it's easy to assume that American culture would have developed ways to support women's participation. Instead, culture is beginning to normalize the image of the exhausted working mom. Expectations for women to manage affairs at home remain.

Although the concepts are not mutually exclusive, work and home do compete for a woman's attention—especially once women have children.[51] Eleanor Roosevelt expressed the tension: "A woman, just like a man, may have a great gift for some particular thing. That does not mean that she must give up the joy of marrying and having a home and children."[52] Roosevelt's words express the battle that is still being fought within many women today. As simple as this concept seems, women find the combination to be, at best, a logistical nightmare. Either women feel compelled to choose one path or the other, *or* they attempt to be a working mother and feel like they have failed as either a mother or a worker, or in both realms. The sense of failure women feel often comes from the limitation of societal expectations and structures.[53]

Interestingly, early Baby Boomers led the women's movement in the 1960s, and they were the first generation of women employed *en masse*. However, this generation of women experienced declining fertility rates as they sought to combine work and family.[54] Earlier generations paved the way for women to "have it all." Women could have both work *and* family. But, if responsibilities at home did not diminish (or were not shared) when a woman chose to work outside the home, she was forced to figure out how to accomplish her duties at work and at home within the boundaries of the same 24-hour day. As comedian Lily Tomlin quipped, "If I had known what it would be like to have it all, I might have been willing to settle for less." The balancing act of work and family for women shapes a different work experience than for men.

Women want sustainable ways to combine work and family. But, when confronted with the realities of doing both, women may feel forced to abandon one or the other. Some women who struggled to prioritize work and family chose to sacrifice in a different way as evidenced by the opt-out revolution.[55] For educated women, *opting out* is a reaction to barriers of the integration of work and family, not a choice among viable options.[56] If opting out is a response to the environment, then the social environment must be better understood. Yet, from this perspective, women who leave the workplace are not *opting* out; rather, they are *pushed out* by a work environment that is hostile to women, children, and the demands of family life. Looking at the wider societal context, women are influenced by a variety of factors when making decisions about work, including cultural expectations about parenting and limited childcare options.

People are products of their societal upbringing, their experiences, their corner of the world. For women, this is evidenced through social norms that have limited their own expectations and aspirations. If women want to see change, they need to stray from those norms (as women pioneers have).[57] Deviant behavior plays an active, constructive role in society by ultimately helping to cohere different populations within a particular society.[58] Deviance is viewed as a way for society to change over time—including *positive* deviance that leads to positive change. Even in terms of gender equity, deviance may not be recognized as positive until after a new equilibrium has been achieved. Women have operated in the domestic sphere for all of recorded history, so for women to break into the professional sphere has required behavior that can be considered socially deviant. Despite significant shifts for women, cultural norms have not yet caught up—equilibrium has not been achieved. The ramifications of this disequilibrium include that the actions of women in the workplace and even more so as leaders are still viewed as behavior that deviates from social norms and expectations. Although deviance can change culture, potential leaders need development and support.

Nurture

Nurturing women into leadership positions may include having models, mentors, and leadership training. Each of these influences have been found to be particularly important for women to advance professionally, but not all women are accorded these opportunities.[59]

To support the next generation of leaders, formal leadership development programs and informal mentorship relationships have been created, promoted, and fostered by men and women in power.[60] The process of mentorship happens when one person, usually someone in a more senior position, guides the development of an entry-level individual.[61] Mentorship has been found to be a key determinant in career success, advancement, and overall job satisfaction.[62] Though considerable time and resources have been invested in mentorship for women, sometimes explicitly to help retain the best female employees, the pipeline continues to "leak" mid- to senior levels of women.[63] Unfortunately, formal or organized mentorship relationships often do not promote personal and career growth.[64] Mentoring relationships are stronger when the mentor and mentee share values, experiences, and outlooks.[65] Additionally, receiving mentorship at the start of a career influences the trajectory of occupational and personal life.[66] However, a woman often struggles to find a professional mentor—particularly to find the right mentor at the beginning of her career.[67]

Mentorship is an indispensable tool, but clearly not all mentoring relationships offer the same quality of professional support. A nuance of mentorship called *sponsorship* has been found to be a critical link for professional success for women.[68] With sponsorship, a mentor goes beyond giving advice and uses influence to advocate for the mentee.[69] Most mentors fulfill a psychosocial function by caring for the relationship and the personal parts of the life of their mentee. Psychosocial support, which generally happens more among women, focuses on self-confidence and professional identity—providing counseling, role modeling, and friendship.[70] A sponsor provides vocational support that helps the mentee advance in their career and guides them through processes—advocating and coaching.

Table 1.1 Concepts, Behaviors, and Change in Structure, Culture, and Nurture.

Strand	Included Concepts	Manifested Behaviors	Suggested Theory for Change
Structure	• Glass ceiling/cliff • Maternal wall • Labyrinth	• Gender bias • Gender discrimination	*Sequencing*
Culture	• Gender roles • Socialization • Second shift	• Work-family balance • Opt-out revolution	*Positive deviance*
Nurture	• Modeling • Mentorship • Support	• Leader development • Networking	*Sponsorship*

Women both underestimate the professional value of sponsorship and struggle to cultivate it effectively.[71] The mindset of women who continue to believe that hard work alone will help them advance overlooks that women, like men, need a person who will connect them to the next promotion—hard work alone will not get them there.[72] Sponsorship is one of the specific ways individuals progress in the workplace and can be a path to promotions and career satisfaction.

Table 1.1 summarizes the discussion of structure, culture, and nurture in the workplace.

Models of Convergence

While certain elements describe and define structure, culture, and nurture, the three categories inevitably overlap in a person's experience. Certain issues are non-exclusive and must be discussed in terms of two or even all three of the strands. Individuals are in the center of the model (in the area where all three strands overlap) because the literature suggests that the individual is constrained or enabled by particular aspects of structure, culture, and nurture in a given context.[73] Each person's experience is a confluence of these three categories—resulting from both empowering and limiting factors. Women experience all three domains to varying degrees. Clearly the three circles cannot become one—there

The Insanity of Equality 15

are structural issues that are not nurturing or may be countercultural by necessity. Even so, nurturing relationships can be built into the structure of an organization, or a culture can exhibit more nurturing characteristics. Thus, Figure 1.1 shows the relationships of the three strands to each other and to the individual.

Although Figure 1.1 illustrates the interconnectedness and overlap of the three strands, it fails to capture the magnitude of each strand. In Figure 1.2, the circles are stacked to illustrate the scale of each category. Culture is shown to be all-encompassing, which suggests that structure and nurture are subsets of culture. In other words, the elements of each category get increasingly more personal as you move from the outside to the inside of the circle in Figure 1.2. Cultural issues are formed in the broader society and affect citizens of a particular region, a country, or even all of humankind. Issues pertaining to the structure are specific to a local organization, but they are affected by broader cultural issues. Elements of nurture are typically more personal and specific to the individual, yet structure and culture influence the need for and approach

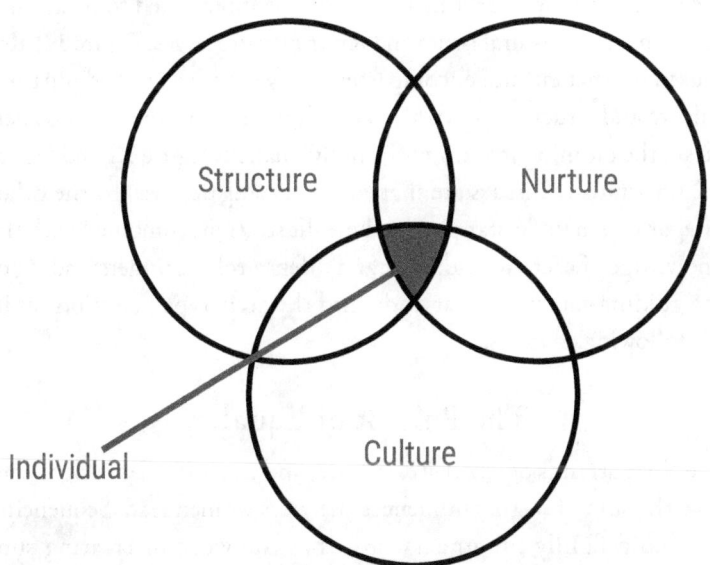

Figure 1.1 The Confluence of Structure, Culture, and Nurture.

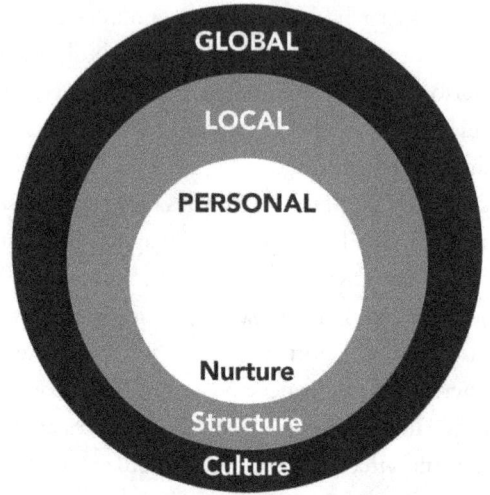

Figure 1.2 The Levels of Structure, Culture, and Nurture.

to nurture. In this model, the individual is at the center at the thickest layer—where the three issues compound. Though the model represents the scale of the strands, this should not be interpreted to mean that there are more cultural issues and fewer nurture issues. Figure 1.2 also illustrates that culture encompasses issues of structure and nurture; culture and structure pervade issues of nurture; all three strands permeate the meaning-making of the individual. As Figure 1.1 and Figure 1.2 illustrate, the issues are shaped (to varying degrees) by the other categories. An understanding of these illustrations combined with the knowledge of each individual strand offers a robust understanding of the guiding categories that undergird the archetypal descriptions in the following chapters.

The Pursuit of Equality

The three strands of structure, culture, and nurture offer insight into how the sum of factors influences the ways women lead. Sequencing work and family life underscores that the work of creating supportive organizational structures for women is not finished. Cultural expectations for the organizational role of women are ahead of actual participation of women. Furthermore, women deviate from the institutional culture by their very presence as well as by their leadership styles. Nurture is the most variable of the three strands because mentorship ranges in involvement from processors to encouragers to sponsors.

Unfortunately, the culture of work *works against* the culture of family. Equality has not and cannot reconcile this discrepancy. Equality is a good tool, yet inadequate, for a task that remains unfinished. Some women convey an overarching care for women's rights and the advancement of women. Other women do not even want to talk about their identity as a woman (in an attempt to neutralize the subject of gender). Still others emphasize their good fortune in becoming a female senior leader. Although women uniquely manage their experiences, three distinct archetypal groups define the primary paths traveled by women into leadership. These women leaders, clustered by emphasis, showed trends across institutional types, age groups, and years of experience.[74] Women, classified as one of three archetypes—Passers, Pushers, or Peacekeepers—differ in their orientations toward leadership but overlap in their determination that moved them *beyond equality*.

CHAPTER TWO

Passers

How Fitting In Is Not Enough

Passers don't mind being one of the guys. In truth, being considered one of the guys means a Passer has made it. Passers grew up with brothers—and measured themselves by their brothers. Passers competed with boys in school. Passers easily engage in conversation about traditionally male topics like sports, cars, or stocks. These women are not intimidated by a room full of men; rather, they discover they belong. Passers survive and succeed because they learn how to blend in rather than distract or differentiate. Women who comprise this first archetypal group learn to "fit" into the male-dominated culture in which they find themselves. These women are Passers.

PASSING IS HOW members of a minority group adopt the language, behavior, and culture of the majority group in order to "pass" as the majority.[1] The theory of passing first developed with race: an African American *passes* for white among her white friends by downplaying her differences. She successfully passes when her friends think of her as like them, so she uses the same phrases, the same body language, the same clothes. Although there are differences as deep as religious beliefs, as superficial as hair products, and as obvious as skin color, a Passer navigates relationships by normalizing herself as part of the majority. Passing extends beyond interracial friendships to age, gender, ethnicity, or class: women passing as men, physically fit persons passing as disabled, slaves passing as free, sinners passing as saints.[2] Although these are untraditional forms of passing, they are not individual attempts to mask their true selves. Rather, these acts symbolize social construction based on cultural forces and personal needs. Symbolic social construction happens not just through words but through clothing, performances, social media presence, and other exchanges that influence beliefs and actions. Some people pass to escape their backgrounds, while others pass as a means of development. In reality, *everyone passes*.

The sought-after American dream is the perfect example of class passing: a hard worker wants to emerge from low socioeconomic status and passes as higher class among those whom he seeks to become. Hollywood movies are full of characters posing as something they are not in hopes of acceptance and gaining entry into the desired group. Chris Gardner is played by Will Smith in the movie *The Pursuit of Happyness*, which is based on a true story of a man who exemplifies passing in his goal to become a stockbroker.[3] He is trapped in the cycle of living paycheck to paycheck, burdened by bills, even evicted from his apartment. In an effort to change the trajectory of his life, Chris secures a job as an intern at a prestigious brokerage firm, but the position does not pay. Chris "passes" in the stockbroker world as a businessman even though financially he is broke and sleeping in shelters. Chris continues to show up to work well-dressed and interacts with coworkers as equals while he privately tries to care for his son's basic needs. At one point, he is homeless and must tote around his possessions; he even brings them to work with him. When he gets odd glances from a coworker, he explains his suitcase and hanging bag by saying that he is going on a work trip, finding relatable expressions that allow him to fit into the intended group (a technique used in passing). Ultimately, his passing pays off—the company sees Chris as "one of them"—and he is awarded a paid position at the firm. Passing allowed Chris Gardner to achieve the American dream.

Passing is not a new phenomenon, but it provides effective language to describe the strategy some women use in the workplace to find fit or to minimize their stigma. Cynthia, a president, observed this pattern of adaptability among her peers:

> When I saw a lot of women in high leadership positions, at a time from maybe a generation before me, at a time when there were very few women in those roles, those women seemed to have taken on more of the male characteristics, and maybe they had to behave that way in order to survive in that world.[4]

Women pass as men so they can enjoy comradery as well as advance in their careers. Sometimes passing extends effortlessly when women are accustomed to being around men. Jasmine, a vice president, attributed her success to her background: "I have spent my entire life with men. I think that gave me a certain skill set. Also, maybe, a thicker skin or a different perspective." Not all Passers are tomboys, but all Passers know how to join the men's conversation. For Passers, adaptability is the means to survive as a woman in a man's world.[5]

Passing comes naturally to Passers. Although a learned response, the behavioral and social modifications often stem from other areas of life. Ann, for example, was generally comfortable among men. She grew up with two older brothers. But she also intentionally took steps to blend in rather than remind others she was the only woman in the room. A quintessential Passer and a vice president, Ann shared that she would study things that interested her male coworkers in order to join the conversation, like learning to talk about football with male colleagues. When the conversation turned from male interests, Ann kept the topics professional in order to avoid topics that might be considered "feminine"—like children, family, fashion, or cooking. Passers have a sense of disdain—even failure—if they are recognized by their peers as a woman or feminine. For some women, their life experiences provided them with existing knowledge on "male" subjects, but other women described studying for these conversations. Evenings and weekends were spent learning NFL conferences and divisions or studying stock jargon. These efforts pay off in the minutes before a meeting when casual conversation turns to football games or the bull market, and women can talk the talk alongside male coworkers.

Passers feel a need to blend in with the guys, which includes looking the part. Passers often standardize their appearance by wearing black or beige suits to appear more like, or pass as, a man. Mary, a president, said, "Earlier in my career, I was always looking for a way to either say, 'I'm not a woman'... to downplay that I was a woman or just to ignore the fact that I was a woman." Physical appearance matters to Passers as a means of gaining acceptance and achieving upward mobility. As Passers advance in their careers, they put less pressure on themselves to be something they are not, yet many of the passing techniques learned earlier continue throughout their careers. Not all archetypes prioritized blending in like Passers.

Over time, Passers begin to view themselves as equals to their male colleagues. Although women senior leaders remain the minority, Passers become accustomed to working among a majority made up of men. Passers are similar to "normal" male administrators and have a higher likelihood of overlooking their gender "stigma" or identity.[6] Women who passed actually succeeded in advancing within a male-dominated system; however, they did encounter systemic barriers. Sydney, a vice president, described her experience: "We adopt the postures, perspectives, understandings about structure and leadership and rules and power through the lens of the white man with whom we work, because we don't yet have real clarity about what the alternative is." Passing as "normal" allows women to act out of a non-stigmatized belief about themselves and, ultimately, navigate beyond equality.

Structure

The architecture of organizations ensures that women encounter more structural obstacles than men do.[7] Even when an organization espouses an ideology of meritocracy—that compensation should be defined by achievement, rather than by gender, race, religion, influence, or socioeconomic status—the enactment of these values is surprisingly slow.[8] In this sense, structure includes persistent gender discrimination and bias in organizational settings, which are impediments to women's advancement.[9] Behaving like men grants Passers structural access not afforded to most women.

One strategy for navigating institutional structural constraints is sequencing—made necessary by sociology and female biology. Women use sequencing to order education, credentialing, marriage, children, family life, and work. Women are the ones who give birth to children, and then, women are the ones expected to put their careers on hold to provide care for children. Sequencing says that women can indeed have it all—just not all at one time.[10]

The prescribed standard biography of young women in the twentieth century was to leave the parental home, marry, and have children before age thirty. However, the standard biography is increasingly being replaced by a choice biography.[11] Suffrage, feminism, and cultural shifts paved the way for individuals to construct their own life course. They may choose to cohabitate before marriage, to parent while unmarried, or to live without children.[12] Personal choices affect the career path of women and result in what sociologists call a de-standardization biography.[13] Additionally, as more women attain higher academic degrees than previous generations of women, studies show that women are delaying marriage and family.[14] This change in timeline may be correlated with the decline in fertility rates in America.[15] Women's divergence from the standard path causes them to encounter more structural barriers in the workforce, but Passers bypassed these structural barriers because they unanimously followed the standard biography.

Passers no longer had children at home. They followed the standard biography—having children earlier in their careers or not having children at all. The decision to have children long before moving into senior leadership allowed Passers freedom and seemingly total commitment to the demanding work of their roles. Alternately, the decision not to have children seemed to provide optimal flexibility for Passers' careers. Passers sequenced to prioritize work in some seasons of life and family in other seasons. However, in periods of emphasizing their careers, Passers prioritized work while dutifully managing the needs of their families, which highlights a Passer's virtue of responsibility.

Career was the primary priority for women in this archetype, but instead of prioritizing career to the detriment or exclusion of family, they operated as a stereotypical breadwinner. Emily explained, "We looked probably like every workaholic couple you've ever seen, or stereotyped, except that I was in the husband role."[16] All Passers were married, with one exception who was divorced, and more than half had children.[17] Passers all described having supportive husbands (significantly more than other archetypes). Having a supportive husband made their work in senior leadership possible. Over and over, women expressed they were "fortunate" to have a supportive spouse and repeatedly used a variation of the phrase: "I could not have done this without him." Support from husbands generally fell into two categories: emotional and practical.

First, emotional support and encouragement boosted women's perspectives and self-efficacy. One dimension of encouragement was marital cooperation rather than rivalry. A woman required a supportive husband so she could channel all her energy toward building her career. Adrienne, a president, shared about her husband, "He was very, very supportive of my career and loved what I was able to do and wanted to assist me in any way possible to make it successful. He was not threatened by my proficiencies." The lack of competition between spouses seemed an important factor for several women. Passers, in particular, thrived when traditional roles were reversed—when her job was the priority. However, sometimes spouses were both in demanding jobs, but they were in different fields. Because wife and husband worked in distinctive industries, the woman did not feel a sense of competition, which allowed the couple to focus on advancing in their individual careers without fear of retribution.

Some women expressed the support of a husband as the result of a long-standing relationship. After decades of married life, Karen, a dean, explained the benefits that accompany a long marriage:

> He kind of knows when things are getting stressful, and he'll pick up extra things around the house, or do dinner.

> He kind of knows, when I am just too tired of making decisions, I'm going to make no decisions at home. That includes, "What do you want for dinner?" I don't know, I don't care, just don't ask me to decide. He does. He'll decide. Part of it is just thirty years of understanding how the other one works.

Particularly for women who had been married for many years, a supportive husband offered them things that they did not even know how to express. Others mentioned understanding husbands when they missed dinner or had a great deal of travel for work. Women with a supportive husband seemed unencumbered by the responsibilities at home—giving them the optimal flexibility and freedom to pursue their work.

Second, support included practical help with domestic responsibilities. Passers specifically praised spouses who were willing to take on household tasks like laundry, dishes, taking the dry cleaning and, especially, care for their children. Although it's not surprising that this tangible help made a difference for Passers, this kind of support opens the door to domestic equality. The need for a practically supportive husband was a recurring sentiment especially among presidents, whose role is arguably the most demanding. Cynthia, a president, said, "I could never do this without his support. I mean, I'm not talking about just moral support, but real, tangible, concrete ... grocery shopping or doing the laundry. When he wanted me to take this position, it was clear that he would definitely be supporting me in this role. That means a lot of things ... all kinds of household duties that I don't necessarily have time for." A posture of support from one spouse motivates the actions of the other spouse. Women leaned on both the emotional and practical support of their husbands to excel in their work. Traditional gender roles and responsibility combined with senior leadership leave women feeling exhausted (if they are even able to advance). A supportive husband freed them to pursue their work—free from judgment and competition at home and free from the full load of domestic responsibilities. Passers were able to prioritize their career because of the cooperation and support of their husbands and through sequencing.

Passers did not just have *supportive* spouses, they had *trailing* spouses who put their own career goals behind those of their wife (in this case).[18] Trailing spouses included men with flexible jobs as well as spouses who had already peaked in their careers. Flexible work, including working in the food industry, teaching, or practicing law, meant that the husband had no difficulty finding a job each time her work moved their family. Women praised the flexibility of their husbands' work. When a spouse had already peaked in his career, women shared that it made it easy to prioritize their own careers. In other words, women sequenced the launch of their career after their husband reached a stable place in his work (in some cases, retirement was on the horizon for the spouse). Melissa, a dean, explained, "He's achieved what he wants to and there's no competition. He sees part of his job as helping me navigate my job, because I'm the one who will continue, hopefully, to advance. He is incredibly supportive." The shift from midlevel work to administration affected the role that women played in their marriage and family. Women expressed personal comfort in pursing their career if their spouse had met his career goals. Rather than equal careers at an equal pace with their husbands, Passers held a turn-taking (or sequencing) mentality with their spouses, which seemed to bypass equality initially, yet offered women an advantage when it was their turn. Equality was not a Passer's goal, yet they did prioritize advancing their career when the timing was right.

One of the right times was when women became empty nesters—all children had flown the coop. "When my youngest kid went off to college, everything changed. My husband decided that he would be the trailing spouse, that my career would be the primary career," Sharon, a president, said. For many women, the transition into administration pushed them into primary financial responsibilities—becoming the main or even the sole "breadwinner." When Sharon began to earn the primary income, she experienced support from her husband. "He was totally okay with it. In fact, I think he really enjoyed it, the freedom, the lack of pressure." When husbands willingly chose to follow their spouse and enjoyed their supportive role, women felt able to thrive in their work.

Culture

America is in the middle of an incomplete gender revolution. Women have achieved new roles and new opportunities, yet women still feel insecure about their place and space in society. Women's Covid-19 shelter-in-place experiences confirmed that women are still the primary caregivers and are typically faced with pressures to put their career on the back burner.[19] However, simultaneously, women's life courses have become increasingly masculinized through career-focused decisions.[20] Passers symbolize the masculinized life course of women. Passers view themselves as "just one of the guys"—a phrase often repeated by women to show that they had successfully assimilated into the culture. Although this action may seem counterproductive for the advancement of women because they are progressing based on their maleness rather than femaleness, Passers used their strategic stealth to forge the way for other women to follow them. Passers play an important role in creating a more comfortable culture for women of different styles to come in behind them.

Passers hold a seemingly evolutionary view of change—that change will happen gradually with little effort needed. Even within hiring, Passers balance a willingness to hire women and a desire for the most qualified candidate for the job. Betty, a president, shared about her approach to hiring: "I look for whoever is best qualified to fill the job. Gender does not enter into that.... I think if everyone does that then we will in time see equity in the number of men and women in positions." As a whole, Passers believe change will happen over time with the "right" practices in place. Passers themselves evolved over the course of their career. For many women who passed earlier in their career, they realized later that their gender was an advantage, not a disadvantage. Because Passers found a way to suppress the nuances of being a woman early in their career as a means of advancement, gender was something they neglected rather than advocated for. Women who passed felt equal to their male colleagues, but they did not express feeling understood or accommodated—which were not even valued by them. Passers believe that their contribution to future women is creating pathways through their own success.

As Passers forged ahead, they experienced being the *first* female: the one who broke through, the exceptional instance, the one different from the others. Sometimes praise erupts upon arrival, but the journey itself is absent of laud. Other times, there is no recognition of the achievement. The moment passes unnoticed perhaps even by the *first*. In reality, *first* feels lonely, wandering, quiet. *First* is often a surprise and not the goal the Passer set out to achieve but an unexpected accomplishment. *First* usually entails a grueling, arduous route without a paved path. The *first* did the next thing without any certainty it would be successful and result in triumph for her and others. *First* requires muscle, inner strength, and perseverance in the face of criticism, resistance, and mockery. When participants were the *first* woman in a role, they fundamentally deviated from what was normal for the institution. "If you're the first woman coming into a job, there will be systems anxiety. It's just the way it is."[21] Passers, in particular, understood the complexities of being a *first*.

Passers were accustomed to being the *first* woman as they ascended to leadership in a male-dominated culture. When asked about their experience as the *first* woman in their role, women typically started listing all of the times they had been a *first*. Women's familiarity with being the *first* did not exempt them from challenges along the way. "Some of these firsts meant I was facing obstacles, because people would question if I was trying to usurp someone else's position, a man's, or if I was really claiming a rightful place," Adrienne, a president, recounted after taking her position in the middle of an institutional crisis. "The school was really about to go under when I began.... The board, I think, expected a miracle worker who looked like a man." As a woman, she broke the mold but ultimately turned things around at the institution—saving it from demise.[22]

Life experience convinced women, Passers in particular, that some differences were irrelevant. Being a woman president was not important to the Passer herself, yet it was a celebration for many people at the institution after having a series of male presidents. When *first* is personified, those watching spout more excitement than the *first* herself. The audience finds a heroine, but the *first* does not feel monumental and meaningful in the moment. Beverly, a college president, shared, "If you think about it, then it feels strange to you. If you focus on it, it can alter your perspective, and in these roles, you cannot ever afford for that to happen, unless it is in a positive way." Passers did not consider their gender as relevant in their professional life. Alexis, also a president, explained, "I've always tried to kind of downplay the fact that I'm a woman leader. It's just: I'm a leader and I do my job. So, I've never really tried to make a big deal out of being the *first* woman." Conceivably, the reality settles in eventually, but initially, the experience is not altered. The *first* proceeds into uncharted territory. In an effort to get where they are going, Passers ignore gender and make it a moot point to the best of their ability.

However, *firsts* mark important occasions for others. Passers expressed a moment (often later in their career) where they realized that their gender did, in fact, matter. "If you are the first or the only, or you're one of a few, you cannot underestimate the importance of what you stand for. I mean, the importance of what that means to people." Alexis recounted, "I've had to sort of look at that through a little bit different lens than I would normally and embrace the fact that I am a woman leader and that it actually mattered . . . and sent a very, very strong message to the broader community." Hope emerges as the *first* brings the expectation of the gate bursting open for more. Confidence stirs as the *first* walks into her destiny. The *first* rarely benefits from her efforts. The reward is the unseen courage inspired in onlookers to faithfully take the next step on the path forged by the *first*.

Nurture

Although structural and cultural factors must align for women, nurture made a notable difference that enabled women to move into senior leadership positions. However, nurture includes various influences from childhood, mentors, sponsors, networks, as well as personal faith, personal health, self-doubt, and a desire to lead. These wide-ranging influences cultivate and curate the style in which Passers lead. While not all leaders rise to leadership in the same way, there are common experiences that enrich leadership. Nurture is unpredictable and all the more influential.

Mentorship encompasses all the different types of supportive relationships women described. When discussing mentors, women commonly used some variation of "I wouldn't be where I am if it were not for them." There was a sense that good fortune or luck played a role in having been mentored. These women experienced mentorship more than the average woman.[23] Most women seemed eager to take whatever mentorship was made available—granted they respected the mentor—and women sought out mentors if they were not readily available.

Women in senior-level administration sought mentors for different reasons, but Nancy, a dean, succinctly put it, "At the most basic level, [mentors] help me not be alone." Higher levels of leadership leave women with fewer colleagues at their home organization in whom they can confide. Thus, loneliness was regularly mentioned as something women felt they had to proactively manage. A few women mentioned mentorship as a tool to combat isolation. Mentors offered both wisdom and companionship. Cynthia, a president, reinforced this idea, saying, "Relationships are critical in everything. You don't get anywhere without having people helping you along the way. Formal mentors or informal mentors, friendships, sounding boards—all of that support—people who cheer you on."[24] Overall, women found mentors to be essential. Mentors all had their own personal styles, but they can be classified into three primary types: encouragers, processors, and sponsors. Passers showed few experiences of processors, some experiences of encouragers, but most of their experiences of mentorship were with sponsors—in contrast with the other archetypes (Pushers and Peacekeepers). However, this should not be surprising because men typically receive sponsorship more than women.[25] Since Passers have learned male behavior, it may be that their adaptation to masculine behaviors was rewarded with sponsorship.

Sponsorship

All archetypes experienced sponsorship, but Passers described more experiences of sponsorship than Pushers or Peacekeepers. Sponsorship helps women achieve the most senior levels of leadership.[26] This special kind of relationship happens when the mentor goes beyond giving feedback and advice and uses his or her influence with senior leaders to advocate for the mentee.[27] More than half of women described a sponsor or advocate who was influential in her journey. "I'm not here (or where I was) without mentors and sponsors." Women defined sponsors as people who "got me on that leadership ladder. They spoke highly of me to different people. I mean, they just promoted me." However, the language of sponsorship was not always used. Sponsors were also labeled as endorsers, advocates, and champions.

Endorsers. A sponsor was characterized as someone who prepared the participant for a future role or career path, even providing a recommendation—either verbal or written. Before moving into leadership, Passers experienced a sponsor earlier in their careers who mentioned their potential for leadership: "I think you'd be a good president someday." Sponsors did not simply make a comment like this and merrily go on their way; it was not an isolated statement. Sponsors both cast vision *and* used their own influence to forge a path for the woman toward that end by providing professional development, "stretch" assignments, or additional responsibilities to nurture necessary skills. For example, Jasmine, a vice president, described an experience with a sponsor who told her, "All right, you need to be a university president. Here are the things I'm going to do to help you get ready." Later in her career, this sponsor challenged her: "When are you going to move out from standing behind these men and find your own role?" This level of candor and assertiveness was common when women described a sponsor. "He pushed me to do more than I thought I could," Jasmine said. This portrayal of sponsors as pushing them along or challenging them was common. Sponsors were distinctively willing to be "brutally honest."

Advocates. Advocacy took many forms: sponsors helping with cover letters; sponsors contributing funding for leadership institutes; sponsors bending rules or breaking tradition to help them advance. Debra, an assistant vice president, explained, "I would attribute the primary doors being opened [for me] to these two women that have just seen in me potential and told me that and talked about opportunities and promoted me and those kinds of things." An advocate empowered her or offered her technical help like coauthoring a publication, appointing her to a leadership role, or providing professional development. This was also a way that women gained self-efficacy. Debra felt it was "important to have someone show that confidence" in her professional abilities. Sponsors took practical actions to help women be successful.

Champions. Many of these women expressed ambition and desire to lead, but the role of the sponsor was to forge a way for the woman. Champions used social sway and political influence to rally support for a person. Passers felt the difference between a mentor and a sponsor. Sponsors, particularly champions, opened a door or created an opportunity for a woman—proactively making a way for a woman to progress in her career. Jasmine said, "You need some mentors, but you also need some champions. In my mind, champions are people who will tell you things that are tough, they will tell you hard truths, they will hold you accountable, and they will push you." In short, sponsors championed women toward advancement.

As may be expected, sponsors do not fit a mold. Sponsors are both men and women. Sponsors are from both formal and informal relationships. Sponsors are both short-term advocates and lifelong champions.

Sponsors enter the picture both early on (even in graduate school), giving them a jumpstart, and later in their careers, giving them a needed boost to a senior-level position. Sponsors emerge through both internal (people at their own institution) and external (people at other institutions) networks, as well as through professional guilds, leadership development programs, and conferences. Despite the different characteristics, the criterion for sponsorship is that the mentor exercises his or her influence in ways that shift the trajectory or accelerate the pace of each woman's career. Passers advanced *because of* sponsors.

The affirmation from sponsors combined with their distinctive poise allowed Passers to progress without self-doubt. Rather than question their ability, Passers were more likely to believe they needed to gain a new skill. A focus on developing skills allows Passers to have a growth mindset, which means they believe that abilities can be developed, as opposed to people with a fixed mindset, who believe that abilities are predetermined.[28] Passers exhibited the characteristic of believing they could learn: "For me, it was always about what do I think I need to know that I don't and how do I fix that."[29] Instead of doubting themselves, Passers looked for self-improvement in the forms of additional training, mentorship, or hard work. People with a growth mindset are more likely to flourish than those with a fixed mindset.[30] As a way to move beyond equality, Passers presented themselves with a characteristically male sense of confidence—they adapted to a normatively masculine culture and were competent in their work, which allowed them to thrive in a male-dominated environment.

Conclusion

With gains made by women in the workplace, Passers may become a relic of the past and not the way forward for future women aspiring to leadership. Yet, Passers represent a distinctive approach to working within the boundaries in which they found themselves, as described in Table 2.1. Passers prioritized their career while navigating family life due to the support of sponsors and trailing husbands. Taking the cards they

Table 2.1 Characteristics Associated with Passers.

Passers	
Philosophy	"One of the guys"
Orientation	Goal-oriented
Approach to change	Adaptive
Defining characteristic	Assertive
Core motivation	Career
Virtue	Responsibility
Institutional types	Collegial (31%), Bureaucratic (33%), Political (33%), and Anarchical (29%)
Self-doubt	Least likely

were dealt—the institutional culture, their own personality, their family obligations—Passers used these elements to create an advantage rather than viewing these elements as weaknesses. Passers found that subtle personal adjustments allowed them to influence the culture in major ways. Equality was not gifted to them, even so they navigated beyond it.

CHAPTER THREE

Pushers

How Sheer Determination Is Not Enough

Pushers know what needs to change, and they are ready to *be* the change. Nothing and no one stands in their way. They pioneer the way for women. This archetypal group, the "Pushers," are the women who propel their institutions toward gender equity. Commonly self-identified feminists, Pushers are a mixed group of women. Some are married or remarried, others are divorced, widowed, or single—in fact, all of the single women in this study were classified as Pushers. Pushers were either older or younger but there was a gap in the 45–60 age range (filled by Passers). A few of the oldest women in this study were on the frontlines in paving the way for women in the workforce—the original fighters for women's rights. The younger group of Pushers represented second- and third-wave feminists.[1]

THE FIRST-GENERATION PUSHERS included women like Pamela, a president, who described her first job working in student life at a university in the 1960s. She recalled "the uprising and all of the campus unrest. It was very galvanizing. They were reorganizing and entering a massive planning process to think about how different the future would be." Pamela was highly involved in the women's rights revolution. She never finished a master's degree or doctorate, but she eventually advanced to the level of presidency, which she held for thirty years. Pamela said that her husband was "the stay-at-home parent for [her] whole career." She represents the older group of Pushers who pioneered a way for women to lead in higher education. Unlike a Passer, Pamela did not take a traditional route through graduate education; she forged her way to the top with only an undergraduate degree. She attributed part of her success to her identity as a woman, which she believed was a central piece of her intrinsic motivation to advance. Pamela was the first woman in the nation to be president at her institutional type—a true pioneer.

The second-generation Pushers are the younger cohort, who represent the resurgence of feminist beliefs. Melissa, a dean in her forties, described herself as "a girly girl," which for her meant that she embraced her femininity and pushed the conventional boundaries. Beyond her "super fun colored" suits, Melissa intentionally talked about her children and brought her children to campus events.

> I am very, very, very unapologetically and visibly a mom. When we did [a basketball event] I got . . . clearance to bring my boys on the court, because I was the only woman out there, and I had my two little kids holding my hands the whole time. Because I wanted every other faculty member to see that you can. . . . You can't have it all, but you can balance it. . . . If we have children coming to my football suite, I will bring my children so they can play with the other kids. I don't apologize for it. . . . I will miss two dinners a week, no more if possible. . . . There are weeks where I'm out of town three nights a week, but it's my goal and everybody understands. If my kid is sick, I'm leaving. I work 80–90 hours a week, so I'm not really going to explain myself.

Melissa planned protected family time into her work schedule in an effort to create work-life balance for herself but also as an example for others. Like other young Pushers, Melissa found it important to be a visible role model for other women. "I know it's helped my female faculty. I know that people feel the most comfortable being a parent, male or female, in my college," Melissa said. Not only do Pushers want to help other women along, but they also want to see real change in policies, and they advocate for equitable environments. Melissa even used the term "pushed" to describe how she had affected policy change at her institution. Pushers indeed do *push* their agenda forward because of their strong convictions. Anna, a president, shared, "When you see inequity, you have to speak up for it. I'm really big into equity and diversity and fairness, it's very important to me." Like Melissa, Anna, and Pamela, Pushers are principle-oriented and driven to aggressively and relentlessly pursue change based on their own persuasions, which highlights their virtue of determination.

Pushers believe they bring a unique and needed perspective to their senior leadership roles. To varying degrees, Pushers believe they see the world differently: think differently, decide differently, act differently. Gloria explained, "Women ask different kinds of questions. . . . I certainly think women's leadership, I think people of color's leadership, not just to be clicking off the box of diversity, provides for a different viewpoint because we've had different experiences." One way that women bring fresh perspective is simply by their presence. Many women mentioned that having a woman in the mix "raises the bar on other people being conscientious" about diversity. Adrienne said it this way, "When women are in the room, the room gets smarter. They bring particular skill sets, and so I think women in higher education, at the executive level, are making a significant impact and improving the quality of the offerings." The presence of women affects how everyone around them works, or, in the words of Sydney, a woman's presence "restructures [and] reorganizes institutional patterns." Unlike Passers, who see themselves as one of the men, Pushers believe that women have a particular role to play that is different from men.

Pushers see women as more attentive to the interpersonal and individual needs of people in the office than their male predecessors in their roles. The belief that women have an added value fuels Pushers' sense of confidence and determination to see change realized. Melissa saw her orientation toward people as an asset to her leadership: "I think one of the things that makes me successful is my desire to know people and to learn about them, and to reflect that learning back to them, making people feel like they matter." Pushers agreed that a woman's perspective was helpful to the organization at large.

Structure

The pursuit of progress parallels organizational behavior theories of change agency. In organizational change, the leadership of a change agent is evidenced through a decision, a commitment to bring about change, and an action that promotes progress in that setting.[2] Pushers operate as change agents in their environment through their commitment to modeling leadership for other women and through their action in sponsoring other women. Change agents can be influential in providing guidance and motivation.[3] Just as change agents play an important role in organizational behavior, Pushers play an important role in positively deviating from the norms to push the organization toward gender equity.[4]

Pushers are vocal about the constraints of the antiquated ideal worker model and the impact of working for two greedy institutions.[5] The ideal worker model continues to be the default standard for good work, but Pushers make concerted efforts to redefine the ideal worker. The American view of the ideal worker is an employee who works at least forty hours a week every week (except two) of the year. As women entered the labor force in mass, the norm, though obsolete, was not adjusted.[6] Shaped by the stereotypical married man with a supportive wife at home, the ideal worker is an outdated idea, further outdated in the wake of the pandemic, but it persists as the default standard for good work. After many businesses offered employees remote work during the pandemic, the view of the ideal worker began to shift. However, women continue to feel their work is measured by that model.[7]

The issues of work-life balance are inseparable from cultural expectations and pressures. The participant with the youngest child (the only participant with a child under age five) understood this complexity all too well. Kiara, a vice president and a Pusher, shared her struggles "with being 100% mom, with being 100% employee, being 100% wife, being an active community citizen, and trying to balance it all." Kiara shared that the struggle extends to all areas of domestic responsibility as a parent of a young child. Pushers and Peacekeepers still had children at home, but Passers did not (all of their children were in college and/or adults). Women who work in leadership positions and have children at home find pressures compounding exponentially. The commitment required for executive administrators is all-encompassing, and the full attention demanded by children, particularly young children, is constant. In other words, work and family are both greedy institutions, and women talked in depth about trying to navigate the needs of both. A greedy institution is one that demands total commitment and full attention, so a woman leader with children works for two greedy institutions.[8]

The double dose of high commitments causes women to be less likely than men to seek additional administrative responsibility or senior leadership roles. Lydia shared that work and family were never perfectly balanced for her: "Sometimes it was much more work focus and sometimes . . . more family focused. But you try to maintain your progress in all of those things to do as good a job as you can at being a parent, being a spouse, and being an employee." Pushers used various strategies to navigate the tension between work and family and the challenges that arose. Pushers brought their children along whenever they could to the extra events required for their job—football games, concerts, picnics, and other campus activities. Margaret, a college president, shared, "I made it clear . . . that if we're going to be spending, you know, a football game lasts forever, four hours on a Saturday, then I want [my kids] to be there."

Visibility is a balancing strategy many Pushers use, which they see as providing a role model for other women. "I wanted every other faculty member to see that . . . you can't have it all, but you can balance it." As the only female in her department when she had children, Melissa, a dean, said, "I didn't have that person or those people to serve as a role model for me. . . . I think when I started being very visible with my family that, as I tell people, you get the whole package, because I'm not anything without them." Pushers flaunt their female identity rather than diminish it or cover it up, which means including their family in work events when possible.

However, sometimes the inclusion of children was a result of the challenges of childcare. Childcare ranged from a nanny to a daycare to family members pitching in. Women wanted to do what was best for their children, but women made different decisions about what "the best" was. Pushers were vulnerable about the tensions of childcare choices. Rebecca, a vice president, said, "I worked insane hours, and it did influence my children, which . . . influenced a decision to send my daughter to boarding school when she went to high school. Because my work was impacting her quality of life." Pushers had to make tough decisions in caring for their family and growing professionally.

Women were clear that children were not obstacles, but they did create challenges and slowed their progress. Pushers wanted to be open and authentic about their struggles and "imbalances" with family life. Faith, a provost, found, "There are always tensions between meeting the needs of your students, meeting the needs of the institution, and meeting the needs of your family. . . . You're always having to make choices." Although work-family tensions were accepted as "part of life," Pushers believe the American culture does not value childrearing— developing citizens and children who have faith and integrity—as important work. Pushers felt personal responsibility to voice their parenting struggles as a means of normalizing the experience for others.

Several women in this study talked about managing the tension between work and family to prevent feeling guilty for being a working mother—often termed "mommy guilt" for working and being away from children. To maintain work and family harmony, women turned down promotions and opportunities, which is more common among women than men.[9] Pushers typically described this behavior as fitting their employment around the needs of their family—due to love, conflict avoidance, gender roles, or lack of an alternative.[10] Nancy, a dean, said, "Organizing everything so that I could get my work done and I could also be with my children . . . and my husband . . . saying 'yes' to some things means saying 'no' to a lot of things. You just have to find your way." Even though navigating work and family is challenging, the consensus was that family is not an "excuse" for subpar performance at work. Pushers prioritize their career and have their eyes set on professional success.

Many women shared how they worked to keep pace with male colleagues. Madison described herself as a "frustrated faculty member" because she had ideas that were overlooked in her department. "My husband, at some point, said, 'You know, you just need to be in charge, because then you can say "yes" to people or say "yes" to your own ideas, or whatever.' So, I give him a lot of credit." She took the plunge and moved into administration, even with young children at home, because of the support and encouragement of her husband. The tension between work and family was difficult for Madison at times.

> One night the five of us were sitting down to dinner and I said, "Okay, I'm leaving tomorrow." And my middle child, who is my mini-me, she's my clone, personality-wise anyway, she says, "You're leaving us again? Mommy, you're always gone." You know, I felt the mommy guilt, right? So, I kind of looked—my husband and I sit on opposite ends of the table, and the kids are down the side—I looked at my husband and my husband looked at our daughter and he goes, "Do you like living in this nice house we live in?" "Well, yeah." "Do you like going to Disney?" "Well, yeah." He went through several questions like that, and he said, "The reason we can do that is because of the job mom has. She doesn't like to leave us, but she's got to do it because this is part of her role, and she's got a very important role, and we're proud of her, and we love her, and we want her to be happy. She's going to come back to us, but we have to let her go." The kids were like, "Oh, okay."

> I told my husband later, I said, "I don't think I've ever loved you more than I did right then, because I was sitting there going,

what do I say to my kids?" But he saved the day by framing it in a way that they got it, without me having to feel horrible about it, right?

Although her example focused on the material benefits Madison was able to provide, the point of the story was to show the deep-rooted support her husband had for the work she did, which gave her strength to overcome the guilt she felt. However, not all Pushers had supportive husbands to help them cope.

A few Pushers were single moms during some of their career and shared about juggling the demands of parenthood and work on their own. Carolyn, a vice president, shared about her nearly two-hour one-way commute with "two little ones" at home, juggling getting them "back and forth to school on a day-in and day-out basis" while she was married, but after years of a long commute to work, Carolyn got tenure, which corresponded with her divorce. As a result, she moved closer to the university and brought her children with her. "Now I traded the travel demands with 100% responsibility . . . in terms of being a single parent. So, I didn't have to go as far, but I had 24/7 responsibility." Pushers pressed forward under difficult circumstances.

In the end, Pushers had few, if any, regrets about working while raising children. Gail said, "I was very, very intentional on giving them time. . . . Each of [my children] says they felt like I put them first. To be fair, I don't know that I always put them first, but they feel like I have, so there you go." Several women mentioned that their own memory of being away differed from the way their children remembered their regular presence, which helped them feel content in the end. Lola expressed that pursuing her career was worth it: "When I've asked my daughters about those times and stuff, they don't regret it. They really admire me. They want to be like me. So, I don't feel guilty in that way." However, Lola expressed that her regular travel and the associated extra work for her husband had taken a toll on their relationship. Pushers recognized the costs and benefits of their work for their family.

Culture

Although one may expect to find Pushers at larger, typically more progressive institutions, they were not present there. Women who pushed for women's rights were predominantly at bureaucratic and collegial institutions and had practically no presence at political and anarchical institutions. Collegial institutions seek consensus, and bureaucratic institutions seek rationality.[11] Thus, the widespread acceptance of women in leadership (representing a cultural change) is difficult to achieve—collegial institutions want complete agreement while bureaucratic institutions want to maintain a functioning system, but these things do not happen quickly. This may explain why women felt they needed to be Pushers in these environments. Lola, a dean at a bureaucratic institution, explained, "A woman in a leadership position on a campus, I think, sends a message, 'We are progressive' to the whole campus. 'We are not just stuck with the white man.'" Lola's explanation makes sense only in an institutional setting where "progressive" is not the typical message being conveyed. At a bureaucratic institution that is characteristically unresponsive to society, Pushers serve to challenge the norms and present an alternative. Correspondingly, collegial institutions are characteristically reluctant to change and are another organizational structure and culture where Pushers find themselves needed. Adrienne, president of a collegial institution, believed that women leaders are needed at this time in history:

> I think it is in many respects the time for women. I think people who've done studies of board constitution, as well as leadership teams that include women, understand that when women are in the room, the room gets smarter. They bring particular skill sets and so I think women in higher ed, at the executive level, are making a significant impact and improving the quality of the offerings.[12]

Pushers, like Adrienne, saw their role as helping their institution catch up with national trends or important movements in higher education.

Pushers felt they *had* to work harder than men to achieve the same things. Seeing themselves as competitive and naturally hard-working, Pushers were up for the challenge. Hard work was both expressed as a requirement and a style. "Some of us women presidents say that we think we work harder than the men do. We give up a lot to make sure we get it the way we think it ought to be."[13] Another way hard work was expressed as a requirement was through caution. A healthy sense of fear existed among women about watching every step. Faith, a provost, talked about this: "You had to be five times better than anybody else. You had to be absolutely unequivocally consistently the most outstanding person ever—just to get the same level of attention as some mediocre male. That's the truth." Women of color felt even more pressure. "I am often and completely aware that it's hard to be a Black woman," said Gloria, explaining the way she had always known she had to work harder:

> I grew up with my mom saying, "You have to be twice as good to be considered equal to your white colleagues." She didn't say that with rancor. She didn't say it with nastiness. It was just a matter-of-fact thing. "You've got to be good at what you do and better, because of the world we live in."

Women felt that they had to work harder in order to achieve the higher standards and combat the additional scrutiny.

Deviance. Pushers' commitment to change flows out of their willingness to deviate from the status quo. Deviants are individuals who want to learn and conform to the values, norms, and expectations of society, but they have not been adequately socialized and they are not committed to the values and norms of society.[14] In this regard, Pushers may be inadequately socialized—or may be simply socialized *differently*. Deviance is an effect of social functions and dysfunctions.[15] Deviant behavior plays an active, constructive role in society by ultimately helping to cohere different populations within a particular society.

Arguably, as long as deviants are present, society attempts to control them by setting social norms for acceptable, expected behavior.[16] Deviance can be a way for society to change over time, and *positive* deviance can lead to positive change, but deviance may not be recognized as positive until after a new equilibrium has been achieved. Women have operated in the domestic sphere for all of recorded history, so for women to break into the professional sphere has required behavior that can be considered socially deviant. Society will adjust for deviance (or changes) and return to a state of equilibrium. The deviant behavior of women entering the workplace is creating a *new* equilibrium for society.[17] Pushers take this task personally as they seek to help society progress.

Nurture

Pushers described experiences of sponsors, processors, and encouragers, but of the three archetypes, they had fewer experiences of mentorship. Pushers' behavior and initiative suggest that they may be slightly more self-sufficient or independent and not require external support at the same level as Peacekeepers and Passers. Naturally relentless in their pursuits, Pushers may not have had or not believed they needed a mentor to motivate or encourage them. Pushers who did experience mentorship typically considered it to be less critical to their success.

Women's groups were most appreciated by Pushers. These groups, exclusive to women, meet for professional support—both informally and formally. Adrienne described a group of six women presidents whom she has met with for the last five years. "We bring case studies out of our places of leadership. We designed it ourselves. We'll spend two-and-a-half days, two times a year, on one another's campuses." This "informal peer counseling," as Adrienne termed it, is a way to seek wisdom from a network of women at the same level. Adrienne was not unique in this experience; other women described similar informal peer groups that met annually, monthly, or even weekly, by phone, over lunch, and both on campus and off—there was quite a variety. Other Pushers were part of lunch groups or other regular meetings with the senior women leaders in their institution or at other similar organizations. The connection among women without the presence of men gave Pushers a freedom they had not experienced in any other professional context.

Women's groups produced informal mentorship opportunities. Mary experienced this informal mentorship in a monthly, interdisciplinary dinner group that she started, which Mary said, "seem[ed] to me to have been the best way, rather than be assigned someone or have some kind of formal apparatus of mentorship. It was groups of women gathering together to talk about things that interested them in light of being a woman." The space that Mary created remained professional, yet the informality allowed for a new level of vulnerability and support. Because most of the women described their professional experiences in a male-dominated context, women's group were a shift from the norm. Kiara evidenced this through her experiences of being in male-dominated groups and offering support to other women:

> When we see a woman in the room, we make sure that we exchange information. We serve as a resource, you know, 'If you need something, let me know. Don't forget about this. There's an easier way to do that.' The women amongst the group have been very supportive of one another.

Thus, women's groups facilitate informal mentorship.

However, other Pushers mentioned formal women's groups and leadership programs for women like the HERS institute, American Council on Education leadership programs, college and university association women leaders' groups, and discipline-specific women's groups. Diana touted the benefits of involvement in women-specific professional development: "I think hearing the experiences of other women have helped me, again, be a better female leader." Donna, a dean, shared her experience in a leadership development program: "It was in an environment and a place where you could really ask questions and discuss challenges. I think in part because it was all women in terms of the classes we had, it felt like a safer environment to ask questions." The makeup of women and men in the room changed the conversation—particularly for women earlier in their profession. Kiara, a young mother and vice president, attended a leadership conference for women:

> They talked about being daughter, mom, sister, chancellor, you know, they talked about all of that and how their male counterparts don't have to think about some of the things that they have to think about. I think that's very true because it is the playing field—it's largely dominated by Caucasian men.

For Kiara, hearing other successful women leaders express struggles similar to her own (even beyond their duties at work) gave her hope and renewed energy for her career.

Conversational openness among an all-women audience allowed a wide range of topics to be discussed honestly. Mary described her experience in a program on women in higher education leadership. The program covered topics that included barriers for women into leadership, available supports, public speaking, handling crises, and even professional dress. Mary said the two-week summer program dealt with "all kinds of things that any leader, but particularly a woman leader, would face." Mary found it helpful to interact with women who had advanced to more senior positions in higher education. "I saw women presidents. I had dinner with women presidents. I began to sit with women leaders on a day-to-day basis and talk about the challenges in a very patriarchal environment of stepping up to the plate to lead both men and women." Not only did these experiences provide in-the-moment support, they also provided lasting friendships for many women. Pushers could draw on their "women's network" to help in particular challenges or crises. Women's groups, over and above traditional mentorship, proved to be a source of strength for Pushers.

Table 3.1 Characteristics Associated with Passers and Pushers.

	Passers	Pushers
Philosophy	"One of the guys"	"One giant leap for womankind"
Orientation	Goal-oriented	Principle-oriented
Approach to change	Adaptive	Relentless
Defining characteristic	Assertive	Aggressive
Core motivation	Career	Women
Virtue	Responsibility	Determination
Institutional types	Collegial (31%), Bureaucratic (33%), Political (33%), and Anarchical (29%)	Collegial (46%), Bureaucratic (42%), Political (0%), and Anarchical (0%)
Self-doubt	Least likely	Mixed

Pushers were passionate about women's rights and advancing gender equity. Pushers led out of their convictions and chose deviance to see change affected.

Table 3.1 compares the characteristics of Pushers and Passers.

CHAPTER FOUR

Peacekeepers

How Playing by the Rules Is Not Enough

Peacekeepers did everything right: They were smart. They attended the top universities and graduate schools in their fields; in fact, they were supremely credentialed. They climbed every rung of the ladder, playing by the rules along the way. They made friends and not enemies. They kept the peace instead of making waves. And the system rewarded their consistent hard work and tireless efforts. They were stealthy in their desire for more responsibility, and they quietly took the reins. Others describe them as sweet, kind, dedicated, loyal, deserving of leadership. They earned their way to a position of leading.

WOMEN IN THIS third group were "Peacekeepers," not to be confused with peacemakers; these women ruled with "an iron fist in a velvet glove," as Diana, a vice president, described. Though archetypally kind, Peacekeepers want to effect change—slowly and gradually, of course—but with a sense of mission and purpose. Peacekeepers are guided by their values and their relationships. Values pervade the Peacekeepers' descriptions of themselves and what is needed in leadership right now. Although seemingly similar to the way Pushers held strong convictions, Peacekeepers' awareness of their values was an internal guide more than an external campaign. "I think one of the roles that's emerging right now is almost like the moral backbone of the university," Joyce, a dean, said. "It's an historic moment. I don't mean that women are more moral than men, I just think we're in a moment where situations and behaviors that have been associated with 'that's just how men are,' I think there's going to be less tolerance for that." Joyce expressed how values drive her but are also being demanded at this point in history.

This kind of leader is much like a diplomat—a product of her anarchical environment.[1] Remarkably, Peacekeepers represented 67 percent of women at political institutions and 71 percent of women at anarchical institutions, which makes it unsurprising that Peacekeepers in this study used symbolism, ritual, and tradition to inspire their constituents.[2] Cynthia, a president at a political institution, explained how the history of her institution as a women's college informed her leadership:

> This institution, in particular, one of their areas of strength and something they do well is give many of these women who come to this university, who have never thought of themselves as leaders, or never have taken any leadership roles, ever—which is the case, by the way of many girls and women, because many times in school the guys will take on the role, the leadership roles, and the girls are happy to support them or sit back.... When they come to this institution, because we only have 10 percent men, there's not enough guys to go around for every leadership position in the different classes, study groups, student body president... so the women have to step up. They learn in various different roles and maybe they fail, but it's failing in a safe environment. So, they learn to find their voices and become real leaders.

In her role as president, Cynthia capitalized on the university's heritage to empower her women students as part of the legacy of the institution. Cynthia clearly understands her role as a storyteller at a political institution, which supports the function of leaders at political institutions to unite the university population through rich history and traditions. Moreover, Cynthia's style of leadership prepares her to lead in an anarchical institution where storytelling as a leader is even more important.

A diplomatic style of leadership, though rule-following, is not passive. Peacekeepers can inspire and rally others under a shared vision, but they must prove themselves and show they have what it takes to get the job done.[3] Many Peacekeepers describe working harder than men to achieve the same ends. "I think you have to work harder to show your credentials and be prepared as a woman," Joyce, a dean, explained. "You're under scrutiny all the time for things." Leaders acting as diplomats are under examination and must demonstrate through the conflict their problem-solving and managing skills.[4]

Structure

Of the three archetypes, Peacekeepers were most likely to hold a doctorate. An emphasis on doctorates may suggest that credentials were an important key for them to move through the system. Peacekeepers, due to their nature, needed credentials whereas Pushers were more likely to advocate for their own way and Passers were more likely to be sponsored. Peacekeepers used their credentials as their advocate. However, women from all three archetypes agreed that a doctorate is important. Trinity described, "I do believe ... getting a doctorate degree is critically important—if you're going to work in higher ed, you've got to have the union card." Peacekeepers needed the credential, and this "union card" served them well.

Peacekeepers valued family over their career, yet of the archetypes, their approach to sequencing was the most likely of the three archetypes to include delaying childbearing until after graduate school or after achieving tenure—twice as likely as either Passers or Pushers to wait to have children. Peacekeepers described themselves as "a bit older"—in their mid-30s—when they had children. The prioritizing of career (including education) before beginning to have children was a common sequence among Peacekeepers. Many women wanted to get established in their careers before adding children to their lives.

Wanting to finish law school first, Ann, who had previously been a vice president, explained her delay. "I had really contributed substantially to that law practice, in terms of hours. I'd work Saturdays, I'd work evenings. 'Cause we were just single, I mean, my husband and I, we didn't have any children, so we could invest a lot of time [in work]." Peacekeepers wanted to make upward progress in their careers before having children.

Women who waited to have children were hoping to accomplish other goals first. "We wanted to make sure we could afford them.... Being young in our careers, we wanted to experience married life with us." Kiara, a vice president, thoroughly explained her and her husband's postponement of children: "We wanted the opportunity to experience careers and whatever they would bring: good, bad, or otherwise. We waited to make sure that we were in a position to be able to give 100% to our family." Though their decisions could be seen as exhibiting responsibility, Peacekeepers were arguably acting out of what they deemed wise rather than simply being responsible. Wisdom guided Peacekeepers' decision-making.

Intentional sequencing of children is in line with the Peacekeeper's wise nature. Donna reflected on how things have changed over the years for women with children:

> I think people did not know how to necessarily appreciate individuals who were trying to balance work and family in the way many women were doing at that time. I mean, most of the men who were faculty members who were married, had somebody at home to take care of the family. So, I didn't have children until after I was tenured, but even then, who's taking care of the children? Who's taking them to doctors' appointments? All those kinds of things were still falling a lot on women in a disproportionate way. I don't think I was the only one. That's changed a lot. So, I think people are much more respectful and conscious, these days, about the need to

balance home and work in a way, whether you're a man or a woman.... Once I had children, it certainly impacted my time on track to associate professor. Trying to juggle all the things one juggles. It was just taking me a little bit longer to get everything done.

Children changed the way women did work. Whether women had children early in their 20s or later in their 30s, the entrance of children added responsibilities and relationships that had to be navigated. Women, as well as their husbands, worked out creative schedules to maximize time with their children. Ann talked about working three-quarter time while her husband worked evenings so they could hand off the children and not have outside childcare for their young children. Several women mentioned working odd hours—either early in the morning or late into the night—while children slept. Other women taught night classes while their husbands worked in the day, or for husband-and-wife professors, they worked to alternate their class schedules so one parent was always available for the children.

Many women touted the flexibility of the professoriate and the benefits for motherhood. In Diana's experience as a faculty member before becoming a vice president, she found work-life balance to be achievable: "I think it's incredibly easy to have kids when you're faculty. I mean, the reality is that it's a great lifestyle for women who are trying to sort of have it all." Similarly, Destiny, a provost, shared about how academia gave her flexibility in her schedule: "When my kids were little, it was a great balance.... If you can't be a full-time faculty member at a community college and balance a family, I don't know where you're going to be able to do it." However, many women expressed that working in administration is very different—much less feasible with small children. Diana advised, "If you're going to try to rise to senior leadership in higher ed, you have to either not have children or your children need to be older, or you need to have a willing partner who is willing to be the lead parent." Diana's comments return to the idea of sequencing and intentional ordering of major life events. Sequencing language was used by Peacekeepers as they sought to make wise decisions throughout their careers.

Even so, some women were managing administration with young children. Peacekeepers, in particular, wanted to avoid the clash of their many roles in the names of peace and the absence of conflict. Peacekeepers worked hard to keep a separation of work and home, which highlights a striking difference from Pushers. Madison—a vice president who had young children as an administrator—had three children under the age of four when she first moved into administration. "We were tired a lot," Madison shared with a laugh. She explained, "I think the key is the kids' ages, and their needs at different times. I mean, when you're a parent, when you make that commitment to have children, it's not something you just kind of do part time. I mean, it's a full-time thing."[5] Like most other women, Madison shared that "in many ways it was harder when they were young, because it was getting up in the middle of the night with them to feed them, or when they were sick or whatever. It's just different the older that they get." Although a handful of Peacekeepers shared stories of being in administration with young children, most Peacekeepers prudently used sequencing to keep family from interfering with their career paths.

Peacekeepers followed the established processes and worked within the systems rather than try to make hasty changes. Even so, family was important enough for women to take time with their children or even time off in the summer. Peacekeepers unabashedly made family-affected decisions. Joyce explained her job transitions and how "every time it's been for family." These women not only kept the peace at work, but there's a sense that they were Peacekeepers at home as well by their commitment to their family's well-being. Peacekeeping was pervasive, not just relegated to their professional persona. Women were interested in keeping the peace as they advanced, which is understandable because most served at large institutions with competing interests.

Culture

Values and relationships guided women in this group. Peacekeepers had a relational orientation that undergirded their strategic ability to negotiate their way to the top. Establishing strong relationships allowed Peacekeepers to keep a pulse on the relational tensions and institutional politics, which strengthened their ability to keep the peace. Diana, a vice president, shared about the relational dimension of her work:

> I think I am much more sensitive to the interpersonal relationships of my own leadership team. I pay attention to things like, "Are people getting their professional development needs met? Am I mentoring the women on my staff, or the women at my university, or other women that I know at the academy? Do I make sure that we're having fun on the job, too?" I think I take a much more nurturing role.

These questions reveal Diana's attentiveness to the multifaceted needs of those on her leadership team. Peacekeepers were more cognizant of the emotional well-being of others, and they were also more likely to embody characteristically feminine qualities like gentleness and humility. Several women, like Diana, described themselves as relational, nurturing, collaborative—complemented by their solid inner strength that allowed them to lead with authority.

One such characteristic is relational awareness. In her role as a vice provost, Debra described her connectedness with others as fundamental to her leadership style. "I have very strong emotional intelligence and ... I am able, in some ways it's a burden, but I am able to kind of look at somebody or be in conversation with somebody and kind of know how they're feeling." Several women described themselves as sensitive to the relational aspect of their work, which included an adaptability to the needs of their coworkers. Julia, a college president, defined her relational style as one that values "the whole person." She explained that she wants employees to work hard, but she said, "I understand that they have families and personal things that are important. It's important for me that they are healthy within their family relationships, that they're healthy spiritually, [and] that they are healthy physically." Peacekeepers believed that relational intentionality was important to each person's ability to do their work as well as to the environment. Diana shared her experience of bringing her relational leadership style to her role of vice president at a new institution:

> When I started here I told my executive assistant, "I want everyone's birthdays put on the calendar." I'd bring in a cake or I'd buy flowers or we'd go out to lunch for somebody's birthday. She's like, "We don't do that here." My assistant provost and I said, "Oh, well, we do now. There's a new sheriff in town." I actually think that they now like it. I think it's become an important part of our culture. I do think that there's an expectation that women will be more nurturing as a woman leader, but . . . in some ways, [it] makes for a more collegial environment.

Diana explained how she deviated from the cultural norms by being herself in a new environment. Her insistence stemmed from her belief that a relational approach was an important way to place value on her colleagues.

Collaboration was by far the most common way for Peacekeepers to describe their leadership style. From an affinity toward working collaboratively to a reputation as a collaborator, women expressed collaboration as central to their approach. "My mantra is collaborate, collaborate, collaborate," Mary said. Women are particularly "good at processing complexity" and figuring out "next steps," as Joyce articulated and research confirms.[6] Collaboration was described in primarily three ways: (1) flattened hierarchy, (2) empowerment, and (3) input or team effort. Not all Peacekeepers who described themselves as collaborative touched on all three pieces. Women in other archetypes also described a collaborative leadership style; however, for Peacekeepers, collaboration was the primary language they used to talk about how they created a culture.

Flattened hierarchy. Flattened hierarchy emerged out of views of their own position within the organization. Destiny explained, "I like to lead by example. . . . I don't expect people to do things that I wouldn't do myself. In other words, there's no job that's beneath me. I expect others to feel the same way. We're all in it together." Some women used organizational structure to describe their style. Adrienne said, "I've kind of flattened the hierarchy, and I see myself more at the bottom of the pyramid, empowering others, rather than at the top of the pyramid. It's a different modality. My org chart has me kind of at the "v" at the bottom." Similarly, Cynthia believed in a more "horizontal-type organization," as she put it. "In other words, I don't think that everything comes up to the one person. . . . I believe that you can empower more people to make decisions at various levels." Cynthia connected a flatter hierarchy to the concept of empowerment. By removing themselves from the top of the pyramid, Peacekeepers avoided the traditionally male style of dominant leadership. Peacekeepers were attracted to the harmony and synergy created by a flat hierarchy.

Empowerment. Women described empowerment as the aspect of their leadership style that seeks to work with others and empower them to do their jobs well. Destiny described herself as "supportive of people," in which she explained that she seeks to empower her subordinates: "I'm open to people's ideas. . . . I don't have to be the smartest person in the room. I like to give people a lot of leeway to do things that need to be done in the way that they think they should be done." Empowerment, as women saw it, accomplished greater participation and confidence among people on their team, which is important because Kiara, like many Peacekeepers, believed "it takes a team to make things happen." Kiara felt her team orientation was an important component of her role as a vice president. Also serving as a vice president, Carolyn explained,

"I tend to give credit to the team versus individually, in the hopes of engendering participation by the folks that work with me. . . . That's the way it should be, I think." Peacekeepers had less desire to be in the limelight and enjoyed elevating others, which had the ancillary effect of creating a peaceful unity among her team.

Empowering people can also lessen the pressure on the leader to do it all. Nikki, a vice president, shared an example of empowering her faculty members to take more responsibility with committee work. "Since that step, I think that my style has been even more consultative and delegating, sharing responsibility, not taking responsibility for having to do it all myself, but yet, at the same time, providing direction and leadership." Empowering others as a greater purpose helped bring focus to their work. Adrienne shared:

> I have grown much more comfortable in collaborating with men, without fearing that they would question my competence, if I'm collaborative. Some people think to be powerful you have to be unilateral. I don't think that's the case. I think collaboration is a sign of strength.

Through her collaborative efforts, Adrienne gathered people around her whom she said "have gifts that I don't have and [I] listen to them. I think I have grown in my capacity to seek wise counsel." In the realm of collaboration, women expressed that both empowerment and input from others helped them make "better" decisions—valuing collective wisdom over personal recognition.

Input. Peacekeepers use more input from their community to make decisions, which is admittedly more "time consuming" but ultimately viewed as worth the extra effort. Mary believed collaboration can "create life, rather than doing it in an insulated way, which often is not very economically feasible and certainly isn't product feasible, because you don't have as good a product as when you collaborate and you get minds around the table." Rather than team leadership, where everyone has equal say, collaborative leadership is expressed as creating "a culture where everybody feels comfortable agreeing, disagreeing—having their say," as Karen, a dean, described. Karen makes clear that at the end of the day, she makes the decision and moves forward—and she expects everyone to be on board.

Several Peacekeepers discussed collaboration as an approach that was not normal for their institutional culture. Melissa, a dean, said, "I am very team-oriented and women tend to be.... That is not what the former dean did. He was a man. That's not a characteristic that most of our male deans have.... That was really absent in my college." Melissa took a gendered stance on collaboration, though not all Peacekeepers did. She went on to say, "I think my college needed a woman's touch." Nancy's story illustrates this tension between gender and leadership style. As the first woman dean at her institution, Nancy was met with some resistance as a collaborative leader. "That's the sort of leadership that the school really, really needed at this time, so that makes a difference. They've never had a collaborative leader before. They've had commanders." Nancy explained that the faculty were unsure how to respond to her style of leadership. "That's caused part of the hubbub, you know, early on with people." Nancy sought to create systems for "listening to each other." She hoped to develop a strategic plan after hearing from the faculty. "We all need to have some buy-in so we will want to do it. We're now well into the strategic planning process and things are much better than they were a year ago." Nancy explained, "People are getting used to my leadership style and what it means to have a collaborative leader. I can still be directive when needed, but most of the time they don't need somebody with an iron fist."

Women viewed themselves as inherently collaborative leaders. As Kimberly, a vice president, said: "I am going to be a team player, and smile, and be collaborative in everything I do. That's part of my DNA, professionally." Collaboration was a defining tenet in their leadership style. Although operating in a male-dominated environment, women Peacekeepers typically did not make extra effort to deviate from the norms of the culture. However, their differences did not go unnoticed in the environment. Nancy explained her experience as the first woman dean at her institution: "If you're the first woman coming into a job, there will be systems anxiety. It's just the way it is." Probably due to the inevitable "systems anxiety," most of the time Peacekeepers worked to maintain the culture, not deviate from it. Also, working within the culture rather than challenging it signals their diplomatic tendency to keep the peace.

Nurture

Many Peacekeepers mentioned being fortunate to make it to their position. Women felt privileged to have found supportive husbands and mentors, to have avoided blatant gender bias, and to have achieved career advancement. Clearly, this was not a false humility but rather a genuine understanding that the path was not smooth for everyone. Peacekeepers were highly aware of those around them—ahead of them, behind them, beside them. Women in this group used their own experiences to help others—particularly with issues of work-life balance. Lydia, a president, said, "as a woman who has raised a family and understands what goes into that, I'm very receptive . . . when people talk to me about those issues." Their perceptiveness was one of their strengths, but also surfaced as self-reflection and regular self-doubt.

Peacekeepers were the most likely to experience regular doubt about their own work. Debra, an assistant provost, expressed, "I am not somebody who is naturally self-confident and just believes that I can do things, there's always been self-doubt about, 'Am I smart? Am I worthy of this position?'" Debra was not alone in her doubt; Peacekeepers experienced regular doubt about "being enough" for the job. Kennedy, a dean, said it this way:

> Sometimes you go really strong and if you come upon a situation that you just really haven't faced, or you . . . I think I'm going along really strong, things are going very well, and again, you say something that's very different, or the

outcomes are not looking as positive as you'd like them to be, that can make you doubt. Is this really the job I should be in? Maybe somebody else would have done this better.

Even as Debra experienced doubt as part of her personality, Kennedy expressed how doubt could be situational and take her by surprise. Either way, Peacekeepers—more so than Pushers or Passers—found that their demanding jobs created doubt in them at times. However, Peacekeepers typically viewed doubt as a strength rather than a weakness.

When Mary was asked about self-doubt, she responded that she doubts herself "about every day." But, she was quick to say, "I push away the doubts when I get up in the morning, because I know I've got to get out there and make it happen." Even with this strategy to start the day with confidence, Mary admitted, "Probably when I get home, today, I think, 'Did I make a good decision?' 'How could I have improved that? What did I say that wasn't quite clear?' 'What decision did I make that wasn't a good decision?'" For Mary, this is not necessarily a negative practice. "Whether it's doubting or reviewing, I mean, I would probably, in a more positive way, say 'When do you reflect on your actions,' which is kind of doubting, I guess, because if you felt like it was all great you wouldn't even reflect on them." As women processed aloud about doubt, they normalized it, justified it, explained it, or reframed it.

For some Peacekeepers, doubt was an "early career" issue while for others doubt persisted. Sydney expressed, "I experienced early on . . . that you're just waiting for the day when they're going to figure out you don't know what you're talking about and that you don't really have anything to say. You're just staying an hour ahead. You know? If that, on most things." Sydney realized that she was not alone in these feelings when she talked openly with seasoned colleagues, who were still "wrestling with confidence and capacity." Sydney explained, "I do think I have the muscles for the work that I do, and I do think I have the fortitude to do what I do. I think I have a constant awareness of the desire to do better. Self-doubt is inherently part of that." Many women describe these feelings using the language of imposter syndrome, which is defined as doubting one's own abilities and feeling like a fraud. However, imposter syndrome fails to capture the persistent microaggressions as well as social expectations of women; imposter syndrome puts the onus on women to deal with the effects.[7] In order to overcome imposter syndrome, women need "an environment that fosters a variety of leadership styles and accepts diverse racial, ethnic, and gender identities."[8] Pamela exemplifies this; her self-doubt persisted "every day, absolutely, every day—I think that's a feature of the socialization of girls." Her whole first year as a president, Pamela said, "I was terrified every day." Though she grew accustomed to the role, doubt continued in some ways. "I don't think it absolutely correlates with gender, but I do think we will often find that women are much more self-questioning than many men." However, Pamela did not see this as a weakness of women: "I think it's a positive. I think that leaders who ask about their own abilities are better leaders than those who don't." Time and again, women reframed doubt as an asset rather than a liability.

Gail also attached self-doubt to gender in that women often discount themselves more than men: "Do other women feel this [self-doubt] at times? Of course. Do men? I doubt it. I think they act out in other ways if they feel unprepared." Gloria considered that it might be connected to gender: "I don't know that it's a particularly woman thing to feel imposter syndrome, but you know, I'm 59, I still struggle with imposter syndrome." Gloria phrased it this way: "Really aware of my deficits, as much as I am aware of my strengths. I try to serve out of my strengths and surround myself with people who can help me fill in my deficits. 'Cause I think that's the best way to lead." The regular doubters primarily saw self-doubt as part of the journey. Other Peacekeepers believed doubt was a product of being the *first* in a position. Donna said, "That may be inherent in being the first in various places, that you doubt yourself. Or, I certainly have over the years." On the other hand, Sharon described it as a product of the position itself: "I realized that most people who are presidents come in with a lot of doubts about themselves. That's just normal. It's normal for women and it's normal for men, and you just tough it out and do what you have to do." Lola, a dean, said that as she advanced and took on more responsibility,

> I realize more and more what I'm not good at, and I think I aspire to be something that no one can be, right? I'm good at everything. I can talk to everybody. I can figure out every situation. I have to remind myself that that's not realistic, that the best thing to do is bring people into a group that can complement and give some of those specifics.

Even for regular doubters, they do not stay in a place of self-doubt. Julia explained her times of self-doubt: "There have been many of those. They're usually more of a fleeting moment. I haven't had a time that I've become depressed or despondent or overwhelmed that lasted long." Even so, Julia acknowledged, "I might wake up in the morning and think, 'Oh dear, this day has got more than I can bear today.'" Women find ways of managing the doubt. For Julia, her faith helped her sort through her times of self-doubt:

> The reason I say that it would be short is because as soon as I get to the Lord, then he would say, "No, you can't do it. But you can do all things through me, because I'm going to give you strength." So, the focus for me just had to be to get beyond my own human limitations.

Personal faith was one of many ways that women coped with or overcame self-doubt. "Sometimes the best thing I can do is to get my ego out of the way," Mary, a college president said. "Make the right decisions that have not so much focus on my ability or lack of ability and just kind of not think about that, just do it, and then trust that the instincts are good and that God is guiding in that process." Focusing on the bigger picture, usually in the context of personal faith, was a strategy used by several regular doubters.

Personal affirmations were another coping mechanism. Madison shared how she talks to herself in these moments. "I talked myself off the ledge. I was like, 'Okay, Madison, you prepared, you don't know everything, but yeah, you know something, you probably know more than these students.' But I got through that first class. Then it was like, 'Oh, I can do this.'" Madison went on to say that this experience recurred with each new job she took. "When I felt that way, it just made me prepare better to make sure I didn't fail, that I didn't embarrass myself or hurt the university or the school or college, or whatever." For Madison, a little bit of self-doubt applied the right amount of pressure to keep her performing her best.

When the doubt became too heavy, women assessed what needed to change to make their work sustainable. Michelle explained that her workload became more than she wanted: "I've been working 60–80 hours a week for most of the last year. That's not super sustainable for a human life. I don't want to do that. So, there's a technical doubting my ability and then there's a 'This is actually really not good.'" Once Michelle realized this was an issue of "pure workload," she signaled to the president, "Something needs to shift so that I don't burnout or have a major medical crisis, or decide to opt for some easier job that I don't want as much." Diana shared her escape route: "There isn't a day, almost a week, that goes by that I don't think about going back to faculty. Like, 'Well, I can just go back to faculty.'" One participant succumbed to this option—opting out of her leadership position for a less intense faculty role. Kayla, a vice president, felt pressured by the sum of her commitments more than by her capacity for her job: "I didn't worry about my actual ability to do the work. It was more around would I have time to do what needed to be done to be successful." Kayla's superiors created very difficult working environments, including behaviors of bullying and bias, which led her to opt out.[9]

> Every job has aspects to it that are unpleasant. When I have those kinds of experiences in an academic context, you know, as a professor and as a researcher, I could easily cope with them. I'd get ticked off or rant and rave to my husband, you know, whatever. But it didn't make me fundamentally question what I was doing. But when I was an administrator, every setback made me think about divorce. When a relationship is

> good and you have an argument over something, okay, you have an argument over that thing and it blows over and you carry on. When a relationship is bad and you have an argument over that same little thing, it's immediately cause for reevaluating the relationship. That's what I felt about my relationship to administration.
>
> Everything that happened, I evaluated in terms of, "Oh, I can't do this anymore." In other spheres of work, like as an academic or in other roles that I've had in other situations, I don't react that way. To me that was a very important sign that I, myself, was not temperamentally cut out for doing this work, because it upset me more than it should. I got overly upset by the setbacks that I had, and I think had I fundamentally been more committed to the path I would have found a way of dealing with it.

After many years in two taxing senior positions in administration, Kayla ultimately stepped back into a faculty role. She is the only participant in this study who took this route, but she was not the only one who had encountered steep difficulties. Nancy was involved in a particularly tumultuous situation at her institution: "I definitely had days where I got up in the morning and said, 'I just can't keep doing this, this is really hard.'" In Nancy's institutional environment, she was being severely questioned by her subordinates within her first year in the position. "I doubted myself at times. Like, 'I don't even know what to do next. I don't know who I can talk to, because they don't know either.'" Nancy struggled to know what to do in her situation, which increased her doubt. "A couple things I did that [others] said to do, just made matters worse. There were times where I just felt completely flummoxed." Particularly in challenging situations, doubt felt inescapable for Peacekeepers, who fundamentally desired harmony.

Peacekeepers also described over two-thirds of the mentorship experiences of a processor, which may highlight a particular need of Peacekeepers for a conversation partner. Kimberly, a vice president, explained, "I just need to tell the story and sometimes just by telling the story again you think about it in a different way." The need for someone to identify with their situation and the boundaries of their role was important for Peacekeepers. One of the primary types of mentors is the Processor, who acts as a confidant with whom a woman can share and process challenging situations or aspects of her work and as a conversation partner with whom a woman can brainstorm or bounce around ideas. Oftentimes, this type of mentor was even a peer. Kelly, a dean, put it this way:

> It is wise, I found, to have friends who've been doing this a while that you can bounce things off of. I was lucky enough to have that, those kinds of mentors, who were happy to jump in and help me think through things and feel through things, and would tell me the truth.

The Processor, often referred to as a sounding board, affords the woman freedom to share about her situation—a liberty generally not granted in her position. Ann, a vice president, characterized a Processor: "You just get a constellation of developmental friendships that serve to be good sounding boards and people who speak on your behalf." Ann had experienced this firsthand. "I've had a mixture of men and women throughout my career who just were generous and took the time to speak words of truth, be prayer partners, give a word of endorsement." Cynthia explained that sounding boards are people with whom "you can bounce ideas and have their feedback" and "someone that [you] can talk to and understand the position and be able to have a dialogue about that." The Processor is also someone who can identify with the context and constraints of the role.

Rather than solutions, women expressed looking for a safe space to process an experience. Kimberly, a vice president, said, "It's not counseling in that formal sense, but it's like peer support, like you're going to be okay." Women found that the simple act of a listening mentor aided in the journey to a solution. However, this type of mentor is not restricted to listening but can reflect with the mentee and determine what the mentee needs from them. Processors helped women externally process the situation, empathized with her struggles, and, if needed, advised out of their own experiences.

Processors offered fresh perspective as Lydia, a college president, expressed: "I think mentors are really important because they often help you to see things about yourself that you might not otherwise see clearly or might for whatever reason maybe not be bold enough to see for yourself." A new point of view helped women grow, as Karen said about her mentor: "He really helped me work through decisions as opposed to just telling me what to do. That helped me grow a lot. It helped me start thinking about different perspectives and implications that I hadn't considered to begin with." Processing implies a process, but for the complex challenges these senior leaders faced, they often lacked a protocol or process. Thus, women found a conversational partner to be helpful, if not essential, to thinking through their situations. Karen explained that her mentor did not solely offer solutions: "More than that, they're somebody to listen to me, and they help me see things for myself. I don't think a mentor really gives you the answer—a mentor helps you find the answer." Mentors who processed situations joined the woman on her own journey and helped her cultivate her own leadership skills.

Networking is another aspect of nurture that played a role in women's professional success. Where good mentorship is viewed as a result of fortune and not of strategic behavior, good networking is viewed as a result of calculated actions. In the absence of sponsors, Peacekeepers, by far, were the most likely of the three archetypes to mention networking; Peacekeepers represented about 60 percent of all the experiences described about both external and internal networking. Several Peacekeepers shared about colleagues that they met at a conference or leadership training. Leadership programs provided networking opportunities across geographical boundaries and institutional types. Relationships established through those programs provided valuable resources throughout the course of women's careers. Some of the mentorship relationships described for Pushers were cultivated through leadership programs, but peer relationships also played a meaningful role. Nikki shared about an association of deans and presidents that had

Table 4.1 Characteristics Associated with Passers, Pushers, and Peacekeepers.

	Passers	Pushers	Peacekeepers
Philosophy	"One of the guys"	"One giant leap for womankind"	One with "an iron fist in a velvet glove"
Orientation	Goal-oriented	Principle-oriented	Relationally oriented
Approach to change	Adaptive	Relentless	Incremental
Defining characteristic	Assertive	Aggressive	Empathetic
Core motivation	Career	Women	Family
Virtue	Responsibility	Determination	Wisdom
Institutional types	Collegial (31%), Bureaucratic (33%), Political (33%), and Anarchical (29%)	Collegial (46%), Bureaucratic (42%), Political (0%), and Anarchical (0%)	Collegial (23%), Bureaucratic (25%), Political (67%), and Anarchical (71%)
Self-doubt	Least likely	Mixed	Most likely

"been extremely valuable." Specifically, she said that "to be able to be in a group that has the same kinds of challenges and to share how are we finding our solutions and ways forward. And, how we help one another through very changing and challenging times." However, most women shared that they do not remain in regular contact but still hold a close relationship. Melissa, a Peacekeeper, explained, "I know in a minute if I need something I could call her. She's awesome." Melissa suggests that her network was valuable even if the ties were weak, which exhibits the strength of weak ties.[10] The theory suggests that weak ties were more likely to offer a sense of connection among people in different groups or organizations than those within the same groups or organizations. Peacekeepers, more than the other archetypes, found the strength of weak ties to be an important part of their success and sustainability.

Peacekeepers exhibited tactful and diplomatic leadership. The virtue of Peacekeepers is their wisdom, which was evident through their awareness of others and presence in complex environments. Women in this group embraced some of their characteristically feminine qualities and revealed an inner strength. For an overview of all three archetypes, see Table 4.1.

CHAPTER FIVE

Beyond Equality
The Ethics of Responsive Agency

Responsive agents take control of their actions in the world. They refuse to be the victim but instead initiate a way forward—working creatively within the constraints of their situation. For responsive agents, there is not one right way, there are many, and they do whatever it takes to find their own way. Their stories do not operate as a map for future women; rather, they represent the road less traveled, the path forged under impossible circumstances. They have pushed through *and* past equality. Responsive agents step into authority fueled by their grit, passion, and independence. Responsive agency is available to all women willing to improvise.

WORKING WOMEN STRUGGLE to see a way beyond equality. Perhaps women do not need a path. Perhaps they need a posture. Culture postures women for failure, moving from greedy institution—work—to greedy institution—family—and back. The pursuit of equality keeps plates filled high and sanity low. Women work toward equality believing it will lead them onward and upward, but even if women experience equality, it fails to deliver the hoped-for rewards: liberation, community, imagination, and success. Instead, women feel isolated, stuck, uninspired, and disappointed. Equality is not the tipping point. Women find freedom from the pursuit of equality by improvising. They do this by abandoning the weight of equality and instead choosing creativity within their contexts. The story of gender is always a story of context.

The freedom found through responsive agency always connects to a particular oppressive context. Passers responded to male-dominated contexts. Pushers responded to restrictive contexts. Peacekeepers responded to divisive, acrimonious contexts. An individual's response is characteristically tied to the institutional environment.[1] Women found agency not *in spite of* but *because of* the barriers and constraints. The constraint becomes a kind of gift.[2] Their situational responses illuminate why the behaviors of the archetypes cannot simply be adopted by any woman hoping to advance in her career. Despite the identity and path women leaders embraced (Passers, Pushers, or Peacekeepers), the analysis of the three profiles reveals that equality is simply not enough. Equality is necessary but insufficient. Passers found that fitting in is not enough; Pushers found that sheer determination is not enough; Peacekeepers found that playing by the rules is not enough. Responsive agency, an embodied theological response to gender oppression, offers a way forward for women looking to advance in the workplace and to move beyond equality. Equality is coming. Yet, if a woman wants to be ready for the dawn of equality, she must set her sights on a new goal. Women's experiences offer a window into power, influence, and possibility—their journeys exhibit a series of innovative choices and imaginative advancement. The archetypes organize the findings, yet not all things fit the patterns perfectly, which points to the individual nature and personal agency in each woman's story.

Forging Her Way to Have It All

Kiara was determined to have it all, but when we talked, she was in the throes of balancing career and family. In her late thirties, Kiara had completed graduate school and progressed in her career, and now she had a young child (not yet school age). She had recently advanced to a demanding vice president role at a bureaucratic university. Caught between two greedy institutions, Kiara expressed the tension and challenges of being a young mother in a high-pressure job. As a Black woman, she felt the effects of being a double minority—race and gender.

However, she seemed fueled rather than defeated by her reality. Kiara had not intended to go into academic administration, but once she had, she felt a duty to other women to effect cultural change for a better future. The places she felt constrained were now the places she pursued, opening doors for those who followed her.

Kiara's personal and professional worlds collided constantly. In fact, she has a kid's desk in her office—complete with pencils, crayons, coloring books, and a tablet—for her child if she needs to be at the office after normal business hours. Although this reflects Kiara's obvious commitment to what she called "family first," she said that the culture of her institution and administration was supportive of family values. "I believe in my heart that if I did not have a president who values family, my ability to be a mom would not be as easy as what it is. It's not always easy, but . . . it's easy compared to what I know it could be." Kiara is committed to modeling for other women how to be a mother and an academic leader because she believes other women feel like they need permission to merge their two worlds.

Networking with other women is another way Kiara has found strength to succeed professionally. Kiara makes it a point to connect with other women at meetings, events, or conferences. "If you see a person who is a double minority, then you're super excited because the playing field is largely dominated by Caucasian men." Women serve as a support for one another and share resources, which Kiara was clear is not usually the case when she works with men:

> If you're in a working group, or if you're supposed to be dividing into working groups, [men] won't say, "Hey, do you want to join this group?" It always has to be, "Hey, can I join you guys and work on this with you?" You have to include yourself, because [the men] will not include you or invite you.

Kiara exuded confidence as she shared stories of taking charge and persevering until she gained respect and acceptance. Kiara possessed a relentless drive to make a difference not just for herself but for future women. Her ruthless determination meant she was not deterred by naysayers or barriers; rather, she worked through them. Yet, she confided that she still questions herself and her ability to balance all of her responsibilities:

> I think you always doubt yourself in some shape, form, or fashion. You will doubt whether or not you're capable. You will doubt whether or not you even want to do it. But when that does happen, then I just remind myself, "Well, you thought you couldn't get here, but you did and you'll do this, too."

Cheering herself on seemed to be an antidote to not having a mentor. Though Kiara could identify some voices that had encouraged her toward academic leadership, she also reflected on the lack of mentorship she had experienced. She filled this void through horizontal relationships with other women in academic leadership and through mentoring younger women in higher education. Kiara sought to empower other women and to raise them up into leadership. "Women have to be confident and still be able to be compassionate and kind. I can't believe I'm saying that, because in most instances I think a woman can be just like a man. [But,] I think that's the beauty of being a woman—you don't have to be just like a man." As Kiara pushed for equality for women, she also recognized that it was insufficient.

Charting Her Path to the Top

Alexis took a traditional path to academic leadership. She married right out of college, and shortly after, she went on for her doctorate. After completing her PhD, she became a faculty member, achieved tenure, and served on many committees. Alexis had senior faculty members along the way who encouraged her to take on administrative roles and at least one even suggested that she would make a great dean someday. Encouragement combined with her interest in administrative tasks led her into academic leadership early in her career. In her various roles, she felt supported by her colleagues. "I never really felt like I was treated differently in that role as an associate dean than anybody else would have been.... If I was, I was too naive to realize that I was experiencing it at the time, which certainly could be the case." All of the other administrators in her department were men, but she felt included as an equal in the group. Part of Alexis's ability to fit in was her decision to intentionally wait to have children. She wanted to complete her doctorate, then get her first job, and then earn tenure. Without having children for over a decade of her early career, Alexis was able to focus on her work and professional advancement.

Although Alexis initially expected to be a faculty member for her whole career, she came to a point of redefining her plans. "Eventually I kind of started thinking about: do I want to stay here forever? Do I want to be a dean somewhere else? Do I want to be a provost? Do I want to be a president?" Through the administrative work that she enjoyed, she employed agency to forge her path toward a presidency. Her decisions became more strategic and goal-oriented: she moved from her assistant dean role to become a dean at a smaller institution and later moved across the country to a deanship at a larger institution. The diversity of her experiences prepared her for becoming the first woman president at a large, political institution. She was hired after the university had endured a difficult season, but her appointment seemed to unify the institution and stir hope in the new administration.

> I've always tried to kind of downplay the fact that I'm a woman leader. It's just: I'm a leader and I do my job. I've never really tried to make a big deal out of being the first woman this or that. So, coming here, it was such a big deal for me to be the first woman president. There's a set of people that thought they would not, in their lifetime, see a woman in that role at [this institution]. So, I've had to sort of look at that through a little bit different lens than I would normally and embrace the

fact that I am a woman leader and that it actually mattered.... Almost anywhere else I would have tried to not make as big of a deal out of it.

Fitting in seemed to come fairly naturally to Alexis. It helped that she was athletic, as well as knowledgeable in a field normally dominated by men. In describing her professional journey, Alexis used genderblind descriptions and felt like the fact she was a woman was of little significance *until* her presidency. Alexis responded to the institution's need for her to acknowledge and even celebrate her gender as significant in her role:

> I've had to embrace the symbolism a bit more than I probably was comfortable with at first. I've had, this is the coolest part, I've had lots of moms come up to me with little girls, saying, "Oh my gosh, my daughter wanted to be a lawyer, now she wants to be a university president." That's like the sweetest thing ever. What kid in the world wants to be a university president? Nobody thinks about that. But now little girls who see a woman in that role think, "Oh, I can do that, and I want to do that."

Alexis found that the people at the institution needed her to acknowledge the significance of a woman rising to the presidency role. So, after years of overlooking her gender, she had to celebrate her gender with those at her university. Of course, not everyone supported a woman in the presidency role. Alexis faced some people who believed she got the job only because she was a woman—particularly because of the circumstances that preceded her arrival at the university. But she felt certain that was not the case and chose to ignore some of the initial negative feedback.

Alexis attributes her success to her support systems. As she advanced, she found it helpful to regularly meet with other women in similar positions. The comradery and community were helpful supports for her. Her husband was also supportive as a trailing spouse in a career that could easily transfer and yield to her opportunities. Feeling supported from family to personal faith to colleagues to constituents affected Alexis' confidence and stamina for her work.

Responding to Hurt with Peace and Progress

Kelly was a reluctant administrator at a political institution—so reluctant, in fact, that she turned down her first offer to be a dean. As she recalled, "I didn't think that would be a good use of my skills." The dean then prompted her, "Well, who else would do it if you didn't?" Rather than take that as a signal for her to step up, Kelly provided the dean with some names. "I asked him to consider talking to those faculty colleagues, and he just waited me out. It was a form of self-preservation at first, and then I discovered I enjoyed it." Even after serving in administration, Kelly had no desire for advancement. Kelly shared that she had been equally hesitant about her current deanship:

> A member of the search committee for the new dean is a friend of mine. My partner and I were in town for meetings, and she just sort of casually mentioned that they were looking for a new dean, which I had heard about. I said, "How are you all going to do that?" She asked if I would be interested, and I very politely cursed her out and then said, "No." But she was very persistent, and eventually, I agreed to put my name in for consideration. Then promptly forgot about it. So, I was a bit taken off guard when I got an email asking me to come and interview.

Kelly explained that her reluctance primarily came from previous job searches that had been hurtful—one, in particular. As a racial minority and a lesbian woman, Kelly faced blatant discrimination. Yet, Kelly has progressed in her career because of her composure and hard work. "I have a fairly high work ethic—much to my family's dismay sometimes but that is part of who I am. I want to get the job done; I want it done well; I want it done fairly. I want it done with consultation, helping people feel as though, and actually to be, a part of the process." Kelly described herself as a non-anxious presence, which is likely a developed response to the resistance she has faced, but it also captures her collaborative style of leadership. Her calmness and lightheartedness put others at ease, a kindness not always gifted to her. She responded to obstacles with patience and perseverance, exhibiting a grit and inner strength.

Wisdom is a high value for Kelly. From early on in her career, she sought colleagues and mentors to process her experiences and glean insights. Although Kelly would call herself a type A personality, she was also very relationally oriented, and she benefited from friendship as well as mentorship. Processing with colleagues and mentors allowed her to persevere through difficult seasons and situations. Now well-established in her career, Kelly's poise and thoughtful responses illuminate her own wisdom. She acknowledged that she's a role model whether or not she wants to be:

> I have tendencies toward wanting to be a Super Woman. I think there are many women who are in my same shoes in that regard. We can see how we have an effect on people's lives and the way an institution runs.

Kelly clarified that "there is a diversity of women... we run the gambit politically, ideologically. I don't think we can be categorized into a monolithic something." Even so, she believes women must carry the concerns of gender, sex, sexuality, race, and class and continue to gradually move things forward for other women in the academy. Full of strong belief yet equally full of empathy, Kelly believes that fostering a healthy university entails "honesty, openness, ability to talk and listen, and a willingness to be persuaded." Her professional journey is characterized by these very elements, which culminate to reveal her diplomatic demeanor alongside her desire for cultural change.

The Dawn of Responsive Agency

Spring dawns in a garden, begging buds into blossoms. A gentle breeze blows the resilient grasses, stirs the leafy branches, ruffles the delicate petals. Beautiful flowers grow out of the dirt. The irises bloom in brilliant purples and the marigolds flower in sunny yellows. The roses release a musky sweetness, different in form yet equally exquisite. Butterflies and birds alike find rewards in flitting from flower to flower. Bees collect the syrupy nectar offered by flowers, cross-pollinating for the reproduction of plant life *and beauty*.[3] Vegetation and creatures are in symbiotic relationship. The trees are well-established, with several low-hanging branches being coaxed up, through, high into the treetops. The garden brims with life, movement, growth, delight.

A woman grasps at hundreds of aspects of how to fulfill her potential—how to respond with agency in her given context. She captures complexities inherent with dialectical tensions, encumbered by weight and lightness, responsibility and freedom, hope and terror. A garden seeks balance within its boundaries. The responsiveness of one to another constructs it: grass to wind, blossom to bee, seed to dirt. As women continue to boldly traverse impossible situations, structures will change and develop, but responsive agency agrees that women can thrive in the here and now. There are two obvious parts of responsive agency: first, responsiveness, which is distinctly imaginative in form and strategically individualized in nature, and second, agency, which is marked by ownership and action. A woman must be or grow into being her own agent within her circumstances. Kiara, Alexis, and Kelly, as well as women throughout history, distinctively exhibit responsive agency as a passageway to prospering. Women can follow in their footsteps yet chart their own path toward flourishing.

Conscious Responsiveness

Inherent to responsiveness is, first, the existence of environmental forces and, second, the conscious awareness of these forces and our relationship to them. In higher education, the forces may include academic departments, students, faculty, administrators, student services, government officials, alumni, or donors. For an individual, the forces may include credentials, experience, service, spouse, children, extended family, or health. Women typically carry a higher domestic load than men,[4] so it is likely that they feel the effects of these forces more than men. Most people blindly respond to these forces, but women academic leaders were not blind to them. Women leaders took notice of the relationship between these forces and their actions, which required intention rather than ignorance.

Each woman deliberately chose *responsiveness* within her context. We see this consciousness in the women highlighted in this chapter. Despite her own misgivings, Alexis responded to her constituents by celebrating with them as the university's first woman president. Kiara responded with creativity as she navigated work and family—she found modern ways to merge her worlds in a way that empowered her to thrive (both as a vice president and as a mother) instead of caving under the demands of the two greedy institutions. Kelly responded to discrimination and hardship with quiet strength, grit, and even humor that propelled her upward in her career. Though wildly different from each other, they each employed strategic agility, which is a concept similar to responsiveness in the field of organizational behavior. Strategic agility illustrates responsiveness through defining a pathway for growth by recognizing and responding to the environment, which pairs a high awareness of context with an evolving strategy.[5] By understanding the needs and ethos of their institution, women can adjust their own tactics. Our attention to the institutional culture is fundamental because the evolution of strategy is driven by that context. Conscious responsiveness comes from a readiness to improvise, which can be as simple as Kiara putting a kid's desk in her office or as complex as Alexis relocating her family across the country for a job opportunity. Women at all points in history have exhibited keen improvisational skills—not neglecting the complexities of the environment. Responsive agency is as old as faith is.[6]

Engaging Agency

Empowerment for women to improvise ought to stir passion and energy. Responsiveness brings women to the doorstep of agency—a contagious, terrifying, exhilarating concept. It's a big ask: women, be your own agents. Women, take the reins. Women, don't settle for equality with men; rise up as a woman. But it's an open invitation for women, and anyone daring enough, to deviate from the norms in society—to take a path *with* resistance—to reject passivity, embrace the environment (even within its constraints), and capitalize on personal strengths for a greater purpose. To think for yourself and in turn gift that freedom to others. Women, in particular, don't need another path or prescription, which hearkens back to more oppressive days. Women need autonomy to live into what they were made for and clearance to forge forward. Research reveals women view themselves as less agentic than men.[7] Whether or not women actually *are* less agentic, women must wake up to the power they yield over their own lives. Eileen M. Collins, who became the first American woman to command a space mission, remembers the moment when she realized her own agency. Eileen's father struggled with alcoholism and her mother battled against mental illness. In her memoir, Eileen shared how she processed those difficulties as a child:

> That winter and spring, I realized that I needed to actively take charge of my life. I couldn't just live passively and let things run their course. I saw firsthand what could happen to two wonderful and loving parents when they let bad choices ruin their lives. That spring, I swore I would never let it happen to me.[8]

Eileen spoke of her parents as if they were victims of their circumstances, and she defined how she intended to live differently and "actively take charge" of her own life— this moment birthed her sense of agency. Without this personal revelation, Eileen believed her path would have probably kept her in Elmira, New York, maybe as a science or math teacher at the public school. But, due to her consciousness of personal agency, Eileen became an aviation pioneer in the Air Force and NASA. Eileen points to this childhood realization as defining the way she wanted to direct her life.

So, if agency can be found as a child, what is the importance of agency for mature women? Women academic leaders are marked by choosing agency—generated from independence, improvisation, and intentionality. Perhaps it was first sparked in them as a child, like Eileeen M. Collins, but they have likely chosen to exercise their agency repeatedly throughout their lives and careers. Our individual actions combine with our experience of those actions and affect the way that opportunities unfold.[9] Alexis exhibited such agency and awareness of the power of her actions even though it was inconvenient for her family at the time. "That was a conscious decision I made. I could have stayed, and I probably could have had my whole career [there], but it would have taken me down a different administrative path." Where there was opportunity, Alexis followed it. She did not passively wait for advancement at her own institution; she purposefully moved where she found open doors. The basics of economics and investment teach us that compound growth is a powerful investing tool because it allows the investor to earn returns on both the original investment and on previously received returns.[10] Over the course of decades, compound growth increases an initial investment exponentially. Similarly, compounding personal agency yields compounding growth over time. The diligent find freedom in their work.[11] For Eileen and Alexis, their determined sense of agency emboldened them to be commanders of their own lives and made upward mobility more possible.

Social psychologists break agency into two parts: minimal agency and narrative agency. The former is a first-order experience of agency, which is an embodied, primitive self-consciousness that is not informed by conceptual thought.[12] The latter is more deliberate and informed by social expectations and goals based on personal beliefs. One such explanation of narrative agency follows:

> There are many situations in which an agent *does* reflectively evaluate or explain her actions in terms of a broader framework: a belief system, history, prior intentions, future plans, and so forth. She makes sense of her actions in terms of *who* she is as a continuous, coherent being, the kinds of rules or principles that she follows, and with the understanding that in order to achieve a goal in the future, she may have to accomplish many smaller goals at appropriate times. Her actions in these cases are the result of conscious, decision-making processes, and these deliberative processes lead her to have a contentful mental state that has a causal link to a particular action or series of actions. . . . She appeals in this case to her narrative self, or the self that she understands herself to be, based on her prior actions, belief system, and the way in which she makes sense of herself as a being over time.[13]

Narrative agency captures the essence of identifying goals and working toward them, yet it does not go so far as to consider the imperative of the context.

Agency is not always flashy or extraordinary, but it certainly requires courage. Women face all kinds of difficulties—being overlooked for promotion, drowning in the demands of their workload, receiving a discouraging medical diagnosis, working through behavioral issues with a child—sometimes in several areas of their lives simultaneously. Womanist studies counter single-axis analysis through the concept of intersectionality to work through the marginalization felt in more than one identity (e.g., being woman *and* being Black).[14] Intersectional identity reveals the complexity of each person's situation by acknowledging that the experiences many women face are not traditionally bounded by a single point of discrimination. Instead, as Kimberlé Crenshaw posits, we "need to account for multiple grounds of identity when considering how the social world is constructed."[15] Intersectionality unveils the multi-dimensional layers affecting a woman's experience.

For many women leaders in higher education, intersectionality comes at the point of being a woman and a mother—motherhood makes their experience double oppressive.[16] Women who succeeded in academic leadership were able to carve out agency (awareness of multiple identities and personal power) and responsiveness (change, deviance, creativity, and contribution). In Kelly's story, she reveals that her intersectional identities included gender, racial minority, and sexual orientation. These identities did not preclude her from success, yet her reality did affect her experience as a university administrator. Even so, her response and actions defined her story. Intersectionality is not an excuse for inaction; rather, it can heighten awareness that fuels a strategic response. Rather than fall prey to a victim mentality, a woman can engage agency to achieve her goals.

Reckoning with Responsive Agency in an Age of Equality

Responsive agency offers an intermingling of action and imagination that provide ways forward for women, but not *the* way, for there is not a one-size-fits-all approach. The empty promise of equality set the goal as sameness, but experience and reality reveal the need for creativity, not uniformity; for diversity, not homogeneity; for beauty, not standardization. Creativity, diversity, and beauty are birthed in responsiveness. Embracing these qualities comes from the freedom found in personal action. Women respond uniquely from each other because they have different goals and desires and different methods for achieving them. Yet, responsive agency emerges across all three archetypes due to a parallel drive or determination. Kiara sought to describe this distinction even in her pursuit of equality for women, "that's the beauty of being a woman—you don't have to be just like a man."

This is not a new theory; rather, it's one that's been available to women from the creation of woman. It's inherent to the way women were formed artistically from the *side* of man—to be in his likeness, equal in worth, yet *distinct* from man.[17] Women, though similar, are intentionally different. However, with the reign of equality, we have traded this characteristic uniqueness for cultural acceptance. While women fight against the system, the very goal of equality (defined as sameness, standardization, equivalence) blocks the way for women to truly flourish.

Responsive agency is inherently improvisational instead of prescriptive and oppressive. Women can embrace innovation through social imagination. The power of re-imagining the role of women and the way forward is an expression of creativity and frees one from societal restraints.[18] For a working woman, social imagining offers an opportunity to reset her operating system. A turn to literature may help in this reimagining. Literature offers female characters who discover their own agency. In Zora Neale Hurston's *Their Eyes Were Watching God*, the main character, Janie, epitomizes a woman's struggle with place and role.[19] Janie is an African American woman living after the abolition of slavery. She is not bound by laws, yet she wrestles against social expectations of a woman's place. As she journeys through marriage and life, Janie learns to reinterpret her concepts of God, inherited from her grandmother who raised her, to help her find her God-given agency that leads to love that is heart-wrenching and life that is enjoyed. Janie's enlightened understanding of her own agency results from the same type of struggle against social expectations that women in the workplace face.[20] For Janie and for women in professional circumstances, responsive agency imagines a better way and then becomes the first step into a better way of life.

Women can conform to the system without question, women can question the system yet find themselves powerless to change it, or women can change the system without personally experiencing the benefits. Kelly exhibited this type of liberative work as she networked with other women and sought cultural progress even as she faced intolerance and even rejection. Being a responsive agent means that there will be moments when you come face to face with discrimination, structural barriers, and toxic cultures whether in an official meeting, a baleful email, or a casual "watercooler" moment. Many academic leaders promote a balanced work-life campus culture, yet higher education as a system is slow to change and people's biases can be entrenched and unwavering.[21] Choosing responsive agency does not eliminate the hardships but gives a higher goal, a deeper motivation, and a persevering posture. If a woman can reset her own way of approach, she can move through the system differently with her newfound sense of agency—unentangled by the system. The change begins in us.

Without an ordained sense of agency, women cannot experience true freedom—the very outcome women desire from their pursuit for parity. Freedom cannot be gifted passively through structural or cultural notions of equality. Liberation is a result of the individual's active participation. Said differently, women must be agents for their own liberation. Women have been hurt by men's misuse of power. So, to reconcile their pain and oppression, women have culturally sought equality, but too many times women try picking up the tools that men have used for years and years.[22] However, equality is not rightly achieved by more misuse of power, nor do women need to employ the same tactics men have used. As Alexis realized, "genderblindness" is not the goal. Furthermore, switching places and becoming the oppressor of men does not achieve the mutuality and unity in diversity that we truly desire. It leads instead to grasping for an empty equality. Women often struggle with how to embrace their own agency to overcome oppression. The work of womanist theologian Emilie Townes, who writes on the cultural production of evil, guides women to seek justice and to rightly subvert the cultural production of gender oppression in the workplace. Townes asserts that we must begin with ourselves:

> Each of us must answer the question: What will we do with the fullness and incompleteness of who we are as we stare down the interior material life of the cultural production of evil? Rather than content ourselves with the belief that the fantastic hegemonic imagination, the motive force behind the cultural production of evil, is a force that sits outside of us, we must answer remembering that we are in a world that

we have helped make. The fantastic hegemonic imagination is deep within us and none of us can escape its influence by simply wishing to do so or thinking that our ontological perch exempts us from its spuming oppressive hierarchies. These hierarchies of age, class, gender, sexual orientation, race, and on and on are held in place by violence, fear, ignorance, acquiescence. The endgame is to win and win it all—status, influence, place, creation. Our world needs a new (or perhaps ancient) vision molded by justice and peace rather than winning and losing if we are to unhinge the cultural production of evil.[23]

Townes reveals a deeper meaning to women's work against, or deviating from, the culture. Women seek justice and peace in order to gift that freedom to other oppressed populations. This liberative approach invites a woman to live unreservedly out of her strengths and giftings for a greater purpose.

Not bound by other requirements, responsive agency is an active leadership orientation to grow and develop, postured toward personal progress for a higher goal. Responsive agency satisfies the distinct human role to respond to the opportunities in front of us by employing our individual giftings for a greater purpose. The idea of meaningful living is intertwined with the long-standing discussions on free will and determinism. The Enlightenment birthed many thinkers who adopted the possibility of personal agency in the face of traditionalists. John Locke set the stage for the Enlightenment by rejecting the power of obligatory tradition and promoting the significance of individual experience. A couple centuries later, the sociologist Talcott Parsons asserted that agency connects to effort as the achieving force.[24] An understanding of agency emerged that affirms the ability of human beings to shape their own circumstances.[25] This conception of agency, guided by an ancient vision,[26] may offer fresh allowance for a woman to take calculated actions for purposeful living—this is the power of personal agency, which is available not just to men but to all.

Responsive agency offers women true liberation from conventional constraints. When women are truly free, they can empower other women to find freedom too. The trouble is that women rarely feel truly free. And, if women are indeed free, they often fail to be aware of their status. But, with some intentionality and awareness, women can foster unity by inviting others into community and out of isolation. Integrating others into their vision promotes further agency:

> The agent makes a choice in the light of reasons disclosed by the deliberative process. This choice is a mental event—what early modern philosophers like Locke would have called a *volition* or exercise of the will.... Reasons for action are considerations which speak in favour of or against one's acting in a certain way. When one acts freely in the light of such reasons, by choosing to act in one way rather than another, one is not *caused* so to choose by certain of those reasons, for then one's action would not be free.[27]

Within this deeper explanation of agency, women can have an active role, fueled by their personal sense of mission and vocation, in producing a desired outcome. A woman walking with responsive agency acts with intention that moves her forward on the trajectory of her choosing (based on her beliefs, convictions, and desires). Some women, like Kiara, have "intentionally been visible," believing that they serve as a role model for other women. "I think our role is . . . helping young ladies understand there are more ways to get here than just the typical way, or the traditional way." The influence of a woman in leadership characteristically puts her on display for others to see her lean into her own strengths and thrive within the constraints of her environment. Out of this responsive agency, others see her creativity in leadership and her liberative spirit, which make a way forward for her and, by extension, for others.

Working women need renewed awareness of their own power to act. Acting outside of the norms, though not outside of reason, may deviate from social expectations, but it is the way women actively take ownership rather than passively await equality. Yet, caution must be exercised when prescribing agency as an antidote to gender parity. Agency has been described as a "slippery" concept by sociologists.[28] German sociologist Max Weber described the "black box of personal agency" because of the elusive nature of the concept of agency. Agency does not inherently contain power, but it can be the force that enables women to turn their behavior into *meaningful* action, which is at the core of most women's desires.[29] Agency offers women room to consider past, future, and present without being restrained by them.

Women's actions ought to be informed by longstanding habits and past precedents while also considering future, alternative possibilities. Agency encompasses more than what has been and what could be; agency allows women to consider contingencies within the moment—what is possible right now. Yet, agency does not always arise in a woman in isolation. Nurture heavily influences this process. Mentors, specifically sponsors, play a role in women being able to recognize their own agency—impacting women's confidence, expectations, and actions. Coupling *responsive* with *agency* intentionally directs a woman to a deeper awareness of how her own strengths, her life experiences, and her present environment empower her for her next step. Responsive agency exercises integrative perspective by equipping women to redefine themselves not according to societal expectations but according to intrinsic purpose (the means for which they were made).[30]

Rising to Responsive Agency

Society has made massive strides from the days when women could not attend institutions of higher learning. Women have faced and continue to face glass ceilings, sticky floors, and maternal walls while persevering through first- and second-generation discrimination.[31] The steps that have been taken ought not to be ignored or forgotten because the victories have been hard-won, and there is still much work to be done. Successful women, like Alexis, Kiara, and Kelly, inspire hope as models and as sponsors in a male-dominated environment of academia.[32] No matter the archetype, institutional type, or life course, these women found ways to forge their own trail and meet (even exceed) their professional aspirations. However, women were navigating a tilted playing field. Leveling the playing field, though necessary, falls short of the goal. Normalizing the presence of women in leadership certainly is a first step, but there are more steps to follow[33]—steps that cannot be specifically prescribed.

Women are not all the same. The archetypes as well as life experience reveal the nuances and differences among women. So, if equality with men is the goal, society works toward more sameness, but reality demands more diversity. The real goal is freedom to live out our giftings and callings within our particular environment. Any of these women placed under different circumstances would have responded based on the needs of that particular situation. Their journeys depended on the structure of their lives and the culture of their institutions, as well as the nurture they received. What these women hold in common is a willingness to take the next step with resilience and responsiveness.

Across all three archetypes, women faced challenges. Women saw systemic issues as hurdles that could be overcome instead of blockades that were impassible; women worked through the existing system. Passers, Pushers, and Peacekeepers navigated through systemic barriers, but ultimately, the removal of these barriers will make the path to senior leadership more accessible to women. The Covid-19 pandemic shocked universities and accelerated change, causing administrators, boards, and faculty to reassess traditional modes and methods.[34] Now, research demands are refashioning the university by transforming each faculty member into an economic engine and pushing them to find third-party funding.[35] At a moment when women leaders are emerging at all levels, the route and path to that leadership is now changing. Yet, universities exhibited great innovation and adaptation. Such a time of transformation in higher education paves the way for women to exhibit responsive agency in order to see creative redefinition of structure, culture, and nurture in academia—a way forward for women to move beyond equality.

Rather than women growing up with defined boundaries confining their abilities, women might grow up with freedom to live a life of their determining.[36] As the American novelist and philosopher Ayn Rand said, "The question isn't who is going to let me; it's who is going to stop me." Although society is still settling on its new norms, women are rising into senior leadership and change is underway. But rather than seeking and settling for equality and culturally prescribed paths, women could courageously choose responsive agency.

APPENDIX 1

Rubric for Classifying Institutions

This table is based on the institutional archetypes identified by Birnbaum in *How Colleges Work*.

Criteria	Collegial	Bureaucratic	Political	Anarchical
Size	• Small • Less than 2,000 students	• Medium • From 2,001 9,999 students	• Large • From 10,000– 19,999 students	• Extra large • More than 20,000 students
Structure	• Flat hierarchy	• Vertical hierarchy	• Separate silos	• Fluid participation
Degrees	• Undergraduate	• Undergraduate • Certifications	• Undergraduate • Master's degrees	• Undergraduate • Master's degrees and doctorates • Professional (law, medicine)
Type of Faculty	• Locals • PhD • Teaching focus • Advisors	• Locals • Master's • Teaching focus • Practitioners	• Locals and Cosmopolitans • PhD • Teaching focus • Researchers	• Cosmopolitans • Prestigious PhD • Research focus
Type of Students	• Residential • Full time • Traditional	• Commuters • Part time • Nontraditional	• Majority live off campus • Some residential • Majority in state	• Diverse (ethnic, religious, political) • Live off campus • In state

Note: *This table is based on qualities that can be assessed from an external perspective.*

APPENDIX 2

Participant Information

	Participant	Position Level	Institution Type	Age Range	Race	First
1.	Gloria	Dean	collegial	51–60	Black	
2.	Sydney	Provost	collegial	41–50	white	
3.	Trinity	Provost	collegial	71–80	white	
4.	Ann	Vice President	collegial	61–70	white	*
5.	Michelle	Vice President	collegial	41–50	white	*
6.	Nikki	Vice President	collegial	61–70	white	
7.	Rebecca	Vice President	collegial	61–70	Black	*
8.	Adrienne	President	collegial	61–70	white	*
9.	Julia	President	collegial	61–70	white	*
10.	Margaret	President	collegial	51–60	white	*
11.	Mary	President	collegial	61–70	white	*
12.	Pamela	President	collegial	71–80	white	*
13.	Sharon	President	collegial	61–70	white	*
14.	Kennedy	Dean	bureaucratic	51–60	white	
15.	Lola	Dean	bureaucratic	51–60	white	
16.	Destiny	Provost	bureaucratic	61–70	white	
17.	Faith	Provost	bureaucratic	61–70	white	*
18.	Diana	Vice President	bureaucratic	51–60	white	*
19.	Jasmine	Vice President	bureaucratic	51–60	white	*
20.	Kiara	Vice President	bureaucratic	31–40	Black	
21.	Madison	Vice President	bureaucratic	51–60	white	*
22.	Anna	President	bureaucratic	61–70	white	*
23.	Betty	President	bureaucratic	51–60	white	*

(Continued)

	Participant	Position Level	Institution Type	Age Range	Race	First
24.	Beverly	President	bureaucratic	61–70	Black	
25.	Gail	President	bureaucratic	61–70	white	*
26.	Emily	Dean	political	41–50	white	*
27.	Joyce	Dean	political	51–60	white	*
28.	Karen	Dean	political	41–50	white	*
29.	Kelly	Dean	political	61–70	Black	
30.	Nancy	Dean	political	61–70	white	*
31.	Debra	Assistant Provost	political	41–50	white	*
32.	Alexis	President	political	51–60	white	*
33.	Cynthia	President	political	51–60	white	
34.	Lydia	President	political	61–70	white	
35.	Cathy	Dean	anarchical	51–60	white	*
36.	Donna	Dean	anarchical	61–70	white	*
37.	Melissa	Dean	anarchical	41–50	white	
38.	Tina	Dean	anarchical	61–70	white	
39.	Carolyn	Vice President	anarchical	61–70	white	
40.	Kayla	Vice President	anarchical	61–70	Jewish	
41.	Kimberly	Vice President	anarchical	41–50	white	

APPENDIX 3

Researcher Positionality Statement

NO RESEARCHER APPROACHES their work without a reason. Something drives the research, and the reader ought to know what those things are. My interest in women leaders stemmed from my own natural inclination toward leadership. From a young age, I led my classmates both formally and informally. In high school, I served in several leadership positions and the trend continued in college as I served in residence life and student governance—ultimately as Student Body President. I felt like my best self when I was leading others. My mom had always worked outside the home, and I sought to be a career woman as well. I planned that I would get married at 27 after establishing myself in a career. However, love interrupted my plans, and instead, I married my charming husband at age 22.

Fast forward to graduate school where I entered the inaugural class in a doctoral program. My husband and I faced quite a few challenges in those first couple of years in my program, including the loss of our first child in the spring of my first year—a perfectly planned academic baby due in early June. I realized that complications in personal life did not alter the demands of graduate school and work. The concept of work-life balance entered my mind as a difficult thing to achieve, but I did not understand the impossibility of it until my daughter was born in my second year of graduate school.

As the first woman in the program to require parental accommodation (maternity leave), I experienced the benefits and the drawbacks of being the pioneer. Although my department and assistantship were generally supportive, the experience was incredibly difficult. I remember returning to class with my two-week-old daughter and wondering how other women had navigated these experiences. My husband, and later other generous friends, would sit outside my three-hour classes caring for our daughter so I could feed her before, during, and/or after class. I quickly became aware of the additional challenges of being a woman in the professional world. Before my daughter was born, I wondered why more women were not in leadership positions; after my daughter was born, I wondered how any woman advanced into leadership positions. Of course, the demands of a newborn clouded my view, but the experience also set me on a course to discover the experiences of women leaders.

My supportive environment was still fraught with the difficulties of caring for an infant—lack of sleep, sickness, nursing, pumping, and constant adjustments. Learning to be a parent while pursuing a doctorate and working twenty hours a week meant there was little time for reading parenting books and interacting with other moms. I realized that no one in my program fully understood my experience and the expectations placed on me by society. Not only was I expected to be an excellent student, I was also expected to be a nurturing full-time mother and wife. Although my husband helped with domestic tasks on occasion, I was the manager of the home. I planned and prepared meals, washed clothes (including cloth diapers) and dishes, cleaned the house, and organized childcare. My husband was happy to help with anything that I asked of him, but even with an involved and hands-on husband (and father), the domestic load fell primarily on me, perhaps by choice or perhaps due to societal norms.

My experiences of juggling the greedy institution of doctoral work alongside the greedy institution of my young family inevitably inform the way I approached this study. Although I sought to hear each woman's story independent of my own, I know that my own experiences shaped my interview questions and my interactions with participants. And, although I tried to listen with an objective ear, my ears are female ears and are tuned to hear things from a woman's perspective. My colleague and dissertation chair, Dr. Nathan Alleman, provided an alternate (and male) perspective, but we usually interpreted participants' experiences in similar ways. Nonetheless, my story of infant loss and birth during my doctorate program influences my perspective. At best, this perspective allowed me to be more understanding and accurate in my interpretation. At worst, this study is colored by the experience of a working mother.

NOTES

PREFACE

1 The question comes to bear: do traditional gender roles and biological characteristics still affect us? Are these structures and terms even a viable way to have discourse around this subject? I posit that they do, and furthermore, seeing where we've come from will help us as we look to where we are going. And so, this book sets out to do that.

   The discussion of gender identity and roles within the household is increasingly complex. No longer is the issue binary nor are all households traditional. With evolving LGBTQ+, the possible identities represented are limitless. In some ways, we are not talking about women in the workplace as much as we are talking about minorities. However, I talk specifically about women because impacts of biology come to bear on a woman's ability to work, and the legacy of our traditional systems still affects us today. Even so, the culture of work can work against family no matter the gender identity. It is most likely that the issues at stake are ones that apply to traditional family units, but they may well apply to anyone with children. Children are not the problem; children are indeed gifts from God, the author and creator of the universe. As you can see, this gets complicated quickly. So in this book, I keep the conversation in binary terms of men and women.

2 Herminia Ibarra, Nancy M. Carter, and Christine Silva, "Why Men Still Get More Promotions Than Women," *Harvard Business Review*, September 1, 2010, https://hbr.org/2010/09/why-men-still-get-more-promotions-than-women; Anthony P. Carnevale, Nicole Smith, and Artem Gulish, "Women Can't Win: Despite Making Educational Gains and Pursuing High Wage Majors, Women Still Earn Less Than Men" (Georgetown University Center on Education and the Workforce, 2018), https://cew.georgetown.edu/cew-reports/genderwagegap/. Carnevale et al. report the educational achievements for women statistically surpass those of men, yet the gender wage gap persists. In other words, access for women

to attend colleges and universities is no longer the holdup in the pipeline. The authors offer "six rules of the game," which are evidenced-based strategies for success, for women to achieve competitive pay with men. Their practical and quippy advice reveals the cultural gaps that need to be reconciled alongside the wage gaps.

3 Samuel Cohn, *Race, Gender, and Discrimination at Work* (Boulder, CO: Westview Press, 2009). Cohn is tactful yet honest about race and gender inequality as he examines the sociological and cultural factors at play. I found his discussion on why women are confined to low-status jobs to be poignant and to provide helpful historical context. For a deeper dive into economics, power, and women, I recommend Cohn and Blumberg's *Gender and Development: The Economic Basis of Women's Power*, which takes a broader, global perspective to studying the roles of women in society.

4 Ellen Hazelkorn, *Rankings and the Reshaping of Higher Education: The Battle for World-Class Excellence* (Basingstoke, Hampshire, GBR: Palgrave Macmillan, 2011); Suzana Koelet et al., "The Timing of Family Commitments in the Early Work Career: Work-Family Trajectories of Young Adults in Flanders," *Demographic Research; Rostock* 32 (June 2015): 657–690. Koelet et al. evaluate the complex interplay of education, family, and work and the female marriage penalty of working as well as managing most of the needs of the family, which they term "family-constrained workers." I do not like framing family as a liability, yet their terminology accurately conveys the tension that working mothers, in particular, experience.

5 True brilliance is found in the accessible and evidence-based work of Gosta Esping-Andersen, *Incomplete Revolution: Adapting Welfare States to Women's New Roles* (Cambridge: Polity Press, 2009). He articulately identifies and explains the unfinished gender revolution and the goal of a new and better equilibrium through social reform.

6 Michael S. Kimmel and Amy B. Aronson, *Men and Masculinities: A Social, Cultural, and Historical Encyclopedia* (ABC-CLIO, 2003), 108. This book is a resource on how masculinity has historically been viewed—not my typical read nor one I recommend. But, it portrays the traditional male role and it opens a dialogue around the cultural characteristics of gender.

7 Prime, "Women 'Take Care,' Men 'Take Charge': Managers' Stereotypic Perceptions of Women and Men Leaders," 2009. This is one of many pieces that highlights the cultural assignment of women as fragile and feeble. My hope is to dismantle the stereotypes rather than reverse the roles or for women to take on "male" characteristics. This report finds stereotyping is a primary cultural and environmental barrier for women.

8 Many news articles highlighted this shift for women during COVID-19. It felt like a step back for women, and in many ways, these reports show that it was. Tim Henderson, "Mothers Are 3 Times More Likely Than Fathers to Have Lost Jobs in Pandemic," news, Stateline, September 28, 2020, https://pew.org/368K5Jm. Amanda Taub, "Pandemic Will 'Take Our Women 10 Years Back' in the Workplace," *New York Times*, September 26, 2020, sec. World, https://www.nytimes.com/2020/09/26/world/covid-women-childcare-equality.html. Misty L. Heggeness and Jason M. Fields, "Working Moms Bear Brunt of Home Schooling While Working During COVID-19," Census.gov, August 18, 2020, https://www.census.gov/library/stories/2020/08/parents-juggle-work-and-child-care-during-pandemic.html.

9 A deeper look at the literature reveals this is not the case. "Pipelines, Pathways, and Institutional Leadership: An Update on the Status of Women in Higher Education" (American Council on Education, 2016), http://www.acenet.edu/news-room/Documents/Higher-Ed-Spotlight-Pipelines-Pathways-and-Institutional-Leadership-Status-of-Women.pdf; Mary Ann Mason, Nicholas H. Wolfinger, and Marc Goulden, *Do Babies Matter? Gender and Family in the Ivory Tower* (New Brunswick, NJ: Rutgers University Press, 2013); Kelly Ward and Lisa Wolf-Wendel, *Academic Motherhood : How Faculty Manage Work and Family* (Piscataway: Rutgers University Press, 2012).

CHAPTER ONE

1 Well, truthfully, in the moment of creation, God created male *and* female in his image. So, women and men began as equals in the imago Dei (Genesis 1:27). But, before long, inequality stole the show. Adam and Eve gave into temptation and sin entered the world. Their act of rebellion broke the covenant with God, brought about the fall of humankind, and changed the course of history. Since then, women have been considered less than men. Inferiority was built into the struggle between Adam and Eve—men and women.

2 "When you grow up as a girl, it is like there are faint chalk lines traced approximately three inches around your entire body at all times, drawn by society and often religion and family and particularly other women, who somehow feel invested in how you behave, as if your actions reflect directly on all womanhood," M. E. Thomas, *Confessions of a Sociopath: A Life Spent Hiding in Plain Sight*, reprint ed. (New York: Crown, 2014).

3 Patricia Cayo Sexton, *Women in Education*, Perspectives in American Education (Bloomington, IN: Phi Delta Kappa Educational Foundation,

1976). Patricia Sexton offers a helpful chronicle of education up to the mid-twentieth century. Though some of her perspectives still seem limiting toward women, she sets the historical scene of men benefiting from education and women not being afforded the same opportunities.

4 Writing on the role of a married woman in the book *Domestic Duties*, Mrs. William Parkes (self-identified by her husband's name) notes among her instructions to women that "the greater part of a woman's life ought to be, and necessarily must be, passed at home." Mrs. William Parkes, *Domestic Duties; or, Instructions to Young Married Ladies* (New York: J. & J. Harper, 1829).

5 E. C. Cuff and G. C. F. Payne, eds., *Perspectives in Sociology*, 2nd ed. (London; Boston: Allen & Unwin, 1984). This is not unrelated to theological debates around egalitarianism and complementarianism, but it is not my desire for our conversation to tackle those long-standing disagreements. Cuff and Payne merely guide us through the sociological landscape.

6 In the early 1800s, American women increasingly chafed against being solely occupied with domestic concerns and feminine behavior, or what historian Barbara Welter named the "Cult of True Womanhood." Women, quietly at first, joined forces to challenge the socially constructed version of the good woman to expand the definition of womanhood. Sexton, *Women in Education*; Barbara Miller Solomon, *In the Company of Educated Women: A History of Women and Higher Education in America* (New Haven: Yale University Press, 1985).

7 Percentages now reveal dominantly female participation all the way through higher education. Since the late 1800s, females have outnumbered males as high school graduates, but women did not have the opportunity to study at the collegiate level. Sexton, *Women in Education*.

8 Christie Farnham, ed., *Women of the American South: A Multicultural Reader* (New York: New York University Press, 1997). Christine Anne Farnham edited this book, which filled in historical gaps about southern women. She highlights the experiences of white and non-white women from Cherokee to Jewish to Black women. This book adds detailed dimension to history rather than painting in vague broad strokes.

9 As of 2022, states Pew Research, women regularly exceed men in college degree completion rates as well as in the labor force. "Women now outnumber men in the U.S. college-educated labor force," Pew Research Center, 2022.

10 Bill Hussar et al., "The Condition of Education 2020. NCES 2020–144," *National Center for Education Statistics* (National Center for Education Statistics, May 2020), https://eric.ed.gov/?id=ED605216. This report has

Notes

recent statistics of education broken down by various markers, gender being an obvious one.

11 From historical to analytical, all of these sources confirm the increased entry of women into the workforce in the last century: Sexton, *Women in Education*; Solomon, *In the Company of Educated Women*; Hussar et al., "The Condition of Education 2020. NCES 2020–144."

12 Women's participation in the labor force operated with evolutionary and revolutionary phases. The first phase lasted from about 1900 to 1920. In the first phase, the majority of women did not work and did not consider work an option. Almost half of single women held jobs, but only 6 percent of married women worked outside the home. Women with children were even less likely to work outside the home. However, the second phase emerged when the political situation necessitated women's involvement in the workforce. Because men were required to leave their jobs to fight in World War II, the labor force participation rate of women reached an all-time high. As Goldin describes it: "Each evolutionary phase, moreover, led to major advances in the field of modern empirical and theoretical labor economics that mirrored the reality of women's changing role." "The Quiet Revolution That Transformed Women's Employment, Education, and Family," Working Paper (National Bureau of Economic Research, January 2006), 3, https://doi.org/10.3386/w11953; U.S. Bureau of Labor Statistics, "Current Population Survey," 2015, https://www.bls.gov/cps/cpsaat11.pdf.

13 Solomon, *In the Company of Educated Women*, 185. Vera Micheles Dean, who was a modern professional, wife, and mother in the 1930s, proclaimed that "no woman should have to make a choice between home and career."

14 U.S. Department of Labor, "Women in the Labor Force," Government, Women in the Labor Force, 2013, https://www.dol.gov/wb/stats/stats_data.htm#mothers. The increase was from 12 percent in 1950 to 70 percent in 2012. Because women's participation in the labor force was such a new phenomenon, statisticians only started tracking the number of working married women with children under age six in 1950. What a shift we have seen since then.

15 Karine Moe and Dianna Shandy, eds., *Glass Ceilings and 100-Hour Couples: What the Opt-Out Phenomenon Can Teach Us about Work and Family* (Athens: University of Georgia Press, 2010), 2. This book is one of the best in this genre. Though it is over a decade later, the trends identified by these two researchers have been further exacerbated in the years that followed up until Covid-19 when everything shifted again. Even so, their deep dive into the "opt-out revolution" was fascinating and revealed the

compounding issues with work and family life and the struggles to balance it all and the impossibility to truly excel in every area simultaneously. One of my favorite features is the way they honor women no matter what choices they made—focusing on their individual resilience rather than a singular path of success. I hope to do the same in this book.

16 Amy Roberson Hayes and Diamond Lee, "Women, Work, and Families during the COVID-19 Pandemic: Examining the Effects of COVID Policies and Looking to the Future," *Journal of Social Issues* 79, no. 3 (June 2022): 1088–1105, https://doi.org/10.1111/josi.12510. Yes, the pandemic changed everything—both halting progress toward equality for women in the workplace and increasing their domestic load. This research proves the anecdotal evidence we initially heard in the news during COVID. Hayes and Lee used an intersectional framework that revealed the structural inequalities and negative impacts on women from a range of backgrounds.

17 Donna, a dean at an anarchical institution. An anarchical institution focuses on the role of symbols (stories, traditions, rituals) in creating meaning for those within the institution. Ethnically, religiously, and politically diverse, anarchical institutions offer the widest range of degrees from undergraduate, graduate, and professional studies. Anarchical institutions usually enroll the highest numbers of students.

18 Ann B. Nattinger, "Promoting the Career Development of Women in Academic Medicine," *Archives of Internal Medicine* 167, no. 4 (February 26, 2007): 323–324, https://doi.org/10.1001/archinte.167.4.323. This article broadened the awareness of the notion of sticky floors. Others, like economists Baert et al., "Do Employer Preferences Contribute to Sticky Floors?" furthered our understanding by showing that women indeed do have a slower start to climbing the job ladder.

19 Bernie D. Jones, ed., *Women Who Opt Out: The Debate over Working Mothers and Work-Family Balance* (NYU Press, 2012), http://www.jstor.org/stable/j.ctt9qg9pg; Moe and Shandy, *Glass Ceilings and 100-Hour Couples*. Both of these books deal with the pressures and tensions women encounter along their professional journeys, particularly when children enter the scene. *Women Who Opt Out* takes an interdisciplinary approach with contributors who share the difficulties women face in the workplace as they attempt to balance work and family.

20 The Pregnancy Discrimination Act of 1978 provides legal protection for women and forbids employers to discriminate against women for pregnancy, childbirth, and related medical conditions.

21 Kayla, a vice president at an anarchical institution.

Notes

22 Emma Hinchlife, "Women Run More than 10% of Fortune 500 Companies for the First Time," *Fortune*, January 12, 2023, https://fortune.com/2023/01/12/fortune-500-companies-ceos-women-10-percent/. My favorite line from this article is that "women as CEOs isn't an oddity anymore . . . it's not the majority, but it's not an oddity." Although "not an oddity" is a strange mark of progress, the article essentially makes the point that the ceiling has cracked.

23 Hinchlife, "Women Run More than 10% of Fortune 500 Companies."

24 American Council on Education, "American College President Study" (American Council on Education, 2017), http://www.acenet.edu/newsroom/Pages/American-College-President-Study.aspx. If you work in higher education, you are likely familiar with this comprehensive study, which is conducted every five years. The in-depth information captured in this survey provides helpful insights into the makeup of the leaders of American colleges and universities.

25 American Council on Education; Catalyst, "Women CEOs of the S&P 500 Companies," Text, Catalyst, August 2017, http://www.catalyst.org/knowledge/women-ceos-sp-500. Catalyst publishes a list of the women CEOs of the S&P 500. As of January 2023, women held 8.2 percent of the CEO positions.

26 Many sources beg the same question (which happens to be the one we're all asking): if the pipeline is full of women, why are women still the minority of leaders? "Pipelines, Pathways, and Institutional Leadership"; "Barriers and Bias: The Status of Women in Leadership," AAUW: Empowering Women Since 1881 (blog), March 2016, http://www.aauw.org/research/barriers-and-bias/; Hillary J. Braun, "How Should We Address the Pipeline Problem?," *Perspectives on Medical Education* 5, no. 2 (April 2016): 75–77, https://doi.org/10.1007/s40037-016-0266-4; Mason, Wolfinger, and Goulden, *Do Babies Matter?*; Jessica K. Paulus et al., "Where Is the Leak in the Pipeline? Investigating Gender Differences in Academic Promotion at an Academic Medical Centre," *Perspectives on Medical Education* 5, no. 2 (April 2016): 125–128, https://doi.org/10.1007/s40037-016-0263-7.

27 Taub, "Pandemic Will 'Take Our Women 10 Years Back' in the Workplace." Many similar news articles were published about six months into the coronavirus pandemic, raising awareness that women were carrying the bulk of the domestic load with children at home and parents working remotely.

28 In Hayes and Lee, "Women, Work, and Families during the COVID-19 Pandemic," we see adverse employment outcomes for mothers and not for

fathers. They also note the current downtick in participation of women in the workplace.

29 Richard J. Petts, Daniel L. Carlson, and Joanna R. Pepin, "A Gendered Pandemic: Childcare, Homeschooling, and Parents' Employment during COVID-19," *Gender, Work & Organization* 28, no. S2 (2021): 515–534, https://doi.org/10.1111/gwao.12614. Kate Power, "The COVID-19 Pandemic Has Increased the Care Burden of Women and Families," *Sustainability: Science, Practice and Policy* 16, no. 1 (December 10, 2020): 67–73, https://doi.org/10.1080/15487733.2020.1776561. From homeschooling demands to the loss of childcare, mothers were the primary caregiver to step into these voids. These studies provide empirical support for the claims of a gendered pandemic—one in which women's unpaid work increased.

30 Mason, Wolfinger, and Goulden, *Do Babies Matter?*; Ward and Wolf-Wendel, *Academic Motherhood*. These two books look particularly at motherhood and academia. *Do Babies Matter?* looks particularly at the generational shift and in turn the cultural shift of women (especially mothers) in academia. Framed as a resource to help faculty navigate work and family, *Academic Motherhood* is based on a longitudinal study of over a hundred women and offers professional and policy recommendations to support faculty with families.

31 Arlie Hochschild and Anne Machung, *The Second Shift: Working Families and the Revolution at Home*, rev. ed. (New York: Penguin Books, 2012); Arlie Hochschild, *The Second Shift: Working Parents and the Revolution at Home* (New York: Viking, 1989). The idea of the "second shift" was a clarifying and revolutionary term to distinguish between the paid "first shift" and the unpaid labor at home.

32 Various sources examine the structural barriers that women face. Michael A. Zarate and Eliot R. Smith, "Person Categorization and Stereotyping," *Social Cognition; New York* 8, no. 2 (June 1990): 161–185, http://dx.doi.org/10.1521/soco.1990.8.2.161; Teresa J. Guess, "The Social Construction of Whiteness: Racism by Intent, Racism by Consequence," *Critical Sociology* 32, no. 4 (July 1, 2006): 649–673, https://doi.org/10.1163/156916306779155199; Robert S. Wyer and Thomas K. Srull, *Handbook of Social Cognition*, 2nd ed. (UK: Psychology Press, 2014); Carol Shakeshaft, *Women in Educational Administration*, updated ed. (Newbury Park, CA: Sage Publications, 1989).

33 Sexton, *Women in Education*, 7.

34 American Council on Education, "ACE Convenes Discussion on Women in Higher Education," *Gender Equity* (blog), July 16, 2012, http://www.

acenet.edu/news-room/Pages/Discussion-Women-Leadership.aspx; Arlene Rossen Cardozo, *Sequencing* (New York: Collier Books, 1989); Alison Cook and Christy Glass, "Above the Glass Ceiling: When Are Women and Racial/Ethnic Minorities Promoted to CEO?" *Strategic Management Journal* 35, no. 7 (July 1, 2014): 1080–1089, https://doi.org/10.1002/smj.2161; Julie Creswell, "Even After the Glass Ceiling Yields, Female Executives Find Shaky Ground," *New York Times*, August 3, 2017, sec. Business Day, https://www.nytimes.com/2017/08/03/business/female-ceos-glass-cliff.html; Herminia Ibarra and Robin J. Ely, "Educate Everyone About Second-Generation Gender Bias," *Harvard Business Review*, August 21, 2013, https://hbr.org/2013/08/educate-everyone-about-second; Michelle K. Ryan and S. Alexander Haslam, "The Glass Cliff: Evidence That Women Are Over-Represented in Precarious Leadership Positions," *British Journal of Management* 16, no. 2 (June 1, 2005): 81–90, https://doi.org/10.1111/j.1467-8551.2005.00433.x.
35 Shakeshaft, *Women in Educational Administration*.
36 Kelline Sue Cox, "Motivational Factors Influencing Women's Decisions to Pursue Upper-Level Administrative Positions in Higher Education" (PhD diss., Kansas State University, 2008).
37 Shakeshaft, *Women in Educational Administration*; "Title VII of the Civil Rights Act of 1964," Government, U.S. Equal Employment Opportunity Commission, 1964, https://www.eeoc.gov/laws/statutes/titlevii.cfm. Congress passed the Equal Pay Act of 1963 and Title VII of the Civil Rights Act of 1964 to prohibit gender discrimination on wages, salaries, and hiring. The Equal Employment Opportunities Act of 1972 furthered these attempts at nondiscrimination by requiring employment reports at federal, state, and local levels. Governmental efforts have been part of a massive effort by American culture to redress what was a systemic and persistent problem of equality and access.
38 Herminia Ibarra, Robin J. Ely, and Deborah M. Kolb, "Women Rising: The Unseen Barriers," *Harvard Business Review*, September 1, 2013, https://hbr.org/2013/09/women-rising-the-unseen-barriers.
39 D. Scott DeRue and Susan J. Ashford, "Who Will Lead and Who Will Follow? A Social Process of Leadership Identity Construction in Organizations," *Academy of Management Review* 35, no. 4 (October 2010): 627–647; Ibarra and Ely, "Educate Everyone About Second-Generation Gender Bias"; Ibarra, Ely, and Kolb, "Women Rising"; Deborah M. Kolb, "Negotiating in the Shadows of Organizations: Gender, Negotiation, and Change," *Ohio State Journal on Dispute Resolution* 28, no. 2 (June 2013): 241–262; Moe and Shandy, *Glass Ceilings and 100-Hour Couples*.

40 Ibarra and Ely, "Educate Everyone About Second-Generation Gender Bias."
41 Guess, "The Social Construction of Whiteness"; Shakeshaft, *Women in Educational Administration*; Wyer and Srull, *Handbook of Social Cognition*; Zarate and Smith, "Person Categorization and Stereotyping."
42 Ibarra and Ely, "Educate Everyone About Second-Generation Gender Bias."
43 Alice Hendrickson Eagly and Linda Lorene Carli, *Through the Labyrinth: The Truth about How Women Become Leaders* (Boston, MA: Harvard Business School Press, 2007). Eagly and Carli suggest thse metaphor of the *labyrinth* to portray the challenges women face as they seek to find a successful route to top positions.
44 Ibarra and Ely, "Educate Everyone About Second-Generation Gender Bias."
45 Robert Birnbaum, *How Colleges Work: The Cybernetics of Academic Organization and Leadership* (Wiley, 1991), 72. Birnbaum's definition of culture informs his typology of institutional cultures, which I have used to frame this study.
46 Petts, Carlson, and Pepin, "A Gendered Pandemic"; Petts, Carlson, and Pepin; "COVID-19's Impact on Women's Employment," McKinsey & Company, March 8, 2021, https://www.mckinsey.com/featured-insights/diversity-and-inclusion/seven-charts-that-show-covid-19s-impact-on-womens-employment; Stephanie Batram-Zantvoort et al., "Maternal Self-Conception and Mental Wellbeing during the First Wave of the COVID-19 Pandemic.," *Frontiers in Global Women's Health* 3 (2022), https://www.frontiersin.org/articles/10.3389/fgwh.2022.878723; Taub, "Pandemic Will 'Take Our Women 10 Years Back' in the Workplace"; Power, "The COVID-19 Pandemic Has Increased the Care Burden of Women and Families."
47 Hochschild and Machung, *The Second Shift*.
48 Moe and Shandy, *Glass Ceilings and 100-Hour Couples*.
49 Hochschild and Machung, *The Second Shift*.
50 Suzanne M. Bianchi et al., "Housework: Who Did, Does or Will Do It, and How Much Does It Matter?" *Social Forces; A Scientific Medium of Social Study and Interpretation* 91, no. 1 (September 1, 2012): 55–63, https://doi.org/10.1093/sf/sos120.
51 Ann Crittenden, *The Price of Motherhood: Why the Most Important Job in the World Is Still the Least Valued*, 10th anniversary edition (New York: Picador, 2010). Crittenden argues that although *women* have been liberated, *mothers* have not. From a multidisciplinary lens, Crittenden

evaluates the structural disadvantages specific to mothers. Her argument is primarily focused on mothers who do not work outside of the home, but her logic stems from the deeply ingrained expectations of the role of women in society and its institutions.
52 Moe and Shandy, *Glass Ceilings and 100-Hour Couples*, 1.
53 Crittenden, *The Price of Motherhood*.
54 Javier García-Manglano, Natalia Nollenberger, and Almudena Sevilla, "Gender, Time-Use, and Fertility Recovery in Industrialized Countries," in *International Encyclopedia of the Social & Behavioral Sciences*, 2015, 775–780, https://doi.org/10.1016/B978-0-08-097086-8.31104-7.
55 Lisa Belkin, "The Opt-Out Revolution," *New York Times*, October 26, 2003, sec. Magazine, https://www.nytimes.com/2003/10/26/magazine/the-opt-out-revolution.html.
56 Jones, *Women Who Opt Out*, 50.
57 Émile Durkheim, *The Division of Labor in Society*, trans. W. D. Halls (New York: Free Press, 1912). Émile Durkheim first introduced the idea of deviance, reasoning that deviance is an effect of social functions and dysfunctions. According to Durkheim, deviant behavior plays an active, constructive role in society by ultimately helping to cohere different populations within a particular society.
58 Durkheim, *The Division of Labor in Society*.
59 Yolanda Cleveland Friday, "The Impact of Mentorship and Sponsorship on the Job Satisfaction of Female Student Affairs Administrators." A World Economic Forum report that looked at corporate practices for gender diversity found that 59 percent of the companies offered mentoring and networking programs and 28 percent offered programs specifically for women.
60 Ann M. Brewer, *Mentoring from a Positive Psychology Perspective: Learning for Mentors and Mentees* (Springer, 2016).
61 Ibarra, Carter, and Silva, "Why Men Still Get More Promotions Than Women"; Savage, Karp, and Logue, "Faculty Mentorship at Colleges and Universities."
62 Friday, "The Impact of Mentorship and Sponsorship on the Job Satisfaction of Female Student Affairs Administrators;" Ibarra, Carter, and Silva, "Why Men Still Get More Promotions Than Women."
63 In a 2008 Catalyst survey of over 4,000 professionals, 83 percent of women and 76 percent of men reported that they had at least one mentor.
64 Georgia T. Chao, Pat M. Walz, and Philip D. Gardner, "Formal and Informal Mentorships: A Comparison on Mentoring Functions and Contrast with Nonmentored Counterparts," *Personnel Psychology;*

Durham 45, no. 3 (Autumn 1992): 619; Ellen A. Fagenson-Eland, "Perceptions of Mentoring Relationships.," *Journal of Vocational Behavior* 51, no. 1 (1997): 29–42; Ibarra, Carter, and Silva, "Why Men Still Get More Promotions Than Women."

65 Tammy D. Allen, Rachel Day, and Elizabeth Lentz, "The Role of Interpersonal Comfort in Mentoring Relationships," *Journal of Career Development* 31, no. 3 (2005): 155–169.

66 Raymond A. Noe, David B. Greenberger, and Sheng Wang, "Mentoring: What We Know and Where We Might Go," in *Research in Personnel and Human Resources Management*, vol. 21 (Leeds: Emerald Group Publishing Limited, 2002), 129–173, https://doi.org/10.1016/S0742-7301(02)21003-8.

67 Ibarra, Carter, and Silva, "Why Men Still Get More Promotions Than Women."

68 Ibarra, Carter, and Silva, "Why Men Still Get More Promotions Than Women."

69 Ibarra, Carter, and Silva, "Why Men Still Get More Promotions Than Women."

70 K. E. Kram, *Mentoring at Work: Developmental Relationships in Organizational Life* (Glenview, IL: Scott, Foresman, 1985); Raymond A. Noe, "An Investigation of the Determinants of Successful Assigned Mentoring Relationships," *Personnel Psychology* 41, no. 3 (1988): 457–479.

71 Sylvia Ann Hewlett et al., "The Sponsor Effect: Breaking through the Last Glass Ceiling" (Boston, MA: Harvard Business School Publishing, December 2010).

72 Hewlett et al., "The Sponsor Effect." Women at companies that offer sponsorship programs are able to gain a competitive advantage.

73 These are sources that back up this idea of the individual being constrained or enabled: Linda L. Carli and Alice H. Eagly, "Women Face a Labyrinth: An Examination of Metaphors for Women Leaders," *Gender in Management: An International Journal* 31, no. 8 (October 27, 2016): 514–527, https://doi.org/10.1108/GM-02-2015-0007; "Barriers and Bias"; American Council on Education, "ACE Convenes Discussion on Women in Higher Education"; "Pipelines, Pathways, and Institutional Leadership."

74 Because access to women senior leaders is limited, I used a combination of purposeful and opportunistic sampling—selecting useful cases as the opportunity arose. The power and value of purposeful sampling comes from the focus on in-depth understanding. The use of a stratified purposive sample ensured that the particular characteristics of each level from

academic dean to president were represented. Women self-identified their race and age. Pseudonyms were used to protect the identity of participants. I conducted personal interviews with forty-one women college leaders representing four different institutional archetypes. Robert Birnbaum's four institutional types (collegial, bureaucratic, political, and anarchical) classify institutions by the culture specific to their archetype. Although this qualitative study did not attempt to control for the wide-ranging institutional cultures, the use of four archetypes was helpful to separate institutions based on certain common cultural features. There was about equal representation from each type of institution. Also, within each institutional archetype, I sought representation from every level of administration included in my definition: deans, provosts, vice presidents, and presidents. I discovered common sequencing patterns, deviation from institutional norms, and several functions of mentorship. Using the three strands of structure, culture, and nurture, I gained insight and understanding of women serving in senior leadership. I used a two-phase coding schema: provisional coding for the first round and then pattern coding for the second round of coding.

CHAPTER TWO

1 Marcia Alesan Dawkins, *Clearly Invisible: Racial Passing and the Color of Cultural Identity* (Waco, TX: Baylor University Press, 2012). This language is not to be confused with gender identity language (LGBTQ+). The women were not becoming men or making physical alterations to look like men; rather, they found this a way to gain acceptance in the group conversationally for professional gains.
2 Dawkins, *Clearly Invisible*.
3 Gabriele Muccino, dir., *The Pursuit of Happyness*, Sony Pictures Releasing, 2006. Although many stories exemplify these concepts, I reference this movie in hopes many have seen it and will be able to visualize the way that Chris "passes" in order to find a better life.
4 Cynthia, a college president, observed this pattern among her peers.
5 Dawkins, *Clearly Invisible*; Erving Goffman, *Stigma: Notes on the Management of Spoiled Identity* (Englewood Cliffs, NJ: Prentice-Hall, 1963). Goffman's work on stigma helps explain the situations that women face when they do not conform to the norms in the workplace.
6 Goffman, *Stigma*, 107. Stigma typically disqualifies the nonconformer from acceptance in the group. However, Passers have found ways to bypass stigma by bolstering their relationship to "normals," as Goffman referred to them.

7 Guess, "The Social Construction of Whiteness"; Ibarra and Ely, "Educate Everyone About Second-Generation Gender Bias"; Shakeshaft, *Women in Educational Administration*; Wyer and Srull, *Handbook of Social Cognition*; Zarate and Smith, "Person Categorization and Stereotyping." Much research has revealed the inherent structural obstacles in organizations. These are a few excellent resources that deal with first- and second-generation bias.

8 Sexton, *Women in Education*, 7. Indeed, changing values is harder than mandating them.

9 American Council on Education, "ACE Convenes Discussion on Women in Higher Education"; Cardozo, *Sequencing*; Cook and Glass, "Above the Glass Ceiling"; Creswell, "Even After the Glass Ceiling Yields, Female Executives Find Shaky Ground"; Ibarra and Ely, "Educate Everyone About Second-Generation Gender Bias"; Ryan and Haslam, "The Glass Cliff." Structural barriers can be broken down into two groups: (1) persistent gender discrimination and bias in organizational settings, and (2) barriers to women's advancement in said organizations, which include glass ceilings, glass cliffs, and sticky floors. These articles address both groups of barriers.

10 Nicole Lynn Kangas, "Forming Families and Careers: The Effects of Family Size, First Birth Timing, and Early Family Aspirations on U.S. Women's Mental Health, Labor Force Participation, and Career Choices" (PhD diss., Stanford University, 2011). Sequencing can be achieved by intentionally prioritizing one sphere over the other at varying intervals. Although most women did not formally plan their careers and then stick to the plan, the ordering of their lives tells more about their sequencing than any life plan could.

11 Tom Kleinepier and Helga A. G. de Valk, "Ethnic Differences in Family Trajectories of Young Adult Women in the Netherlands: Timing and Sequencing of Events," *Demographic Research; Rostock* 35 (December 2016): 675. The choice biography has grown as the dominant path, which most of us have anecdotal evidence of, but this study provides hard facts that young adult women in the Netherlands are operating based on the choice biography. For the Dutch women in this study, the choice biography looked like opting for premarital cohabiting and delaying marriage. It may look different for your neighbor, but the overarching pathway is not the standard biography.

12 Hilde Bras, Aart C. Liefbroer, and Cees H. Elzinga, "Standardization of Pathways to Adulthood? An Analysis of Dutch Cohorts Born Between 1850 and 1900," *Demography* 47, no. 4 (November 2010): 1013–1034.

Bras et al. found major shifts in the pathways to adulthood. They noted how "societal changes affect life courses as a whole, influencing not just the timing of separate transitions but their sequencing and spacing as well."

13 Kleinepier and de Valk, "Ethnic Differences in Family Trajectories of Young Adult Women in the Netherlands."

14 Jinyoung Hwang and Jong Ha Lee, "Women's Education and the Timing and Level of Fertility," *International Journal of Social Economics* 41, no. 9 (August 19, 2014): 862–874, https://doi.org/10.1108/IJSE-06-2013-0153; Kangas, "Forming Families and Careers"; Kleinepier and de Valk, "Ethnic Differences in Family Trajectories of Young Adult Women in the Netherlands." These articles confirm that women are delaying marriage and family life—seeking education or career goals before family goals.

15 Hwang and Lee, "Women's Education and the Timing and Level of Fertility." Women's education and employment are found to increase the age at which a woman has her first child, which decreases the total fertility rates. "Fertility decline is a shift of childbearing to older ages. The delay of child birth or family formation is the major cause of the recent fertility decline, because a late women's age at first birth reduces the chances of having any further children" (862).

16 Emily, a dean at a political institution.

17 About 62 percent of Passers had children.

18 Eighty-five percent of Passers had trailing spouses.

19 Petts, Carlson, and Pepin, "A Gendered Pandemic." Considering the cultural impact of COVID-19 on the work of a woman is relevant to the conversation on women in the workplace. COVID-19 revealed some of the places in the home sphere where women carry a heavier load.

20 Esping-Andersen, *Incomplete Revolution*. In studying the contemporary shifts for women in higher education, I conceptualize the effort toward equality as a process that, through action and re-action, gradually produces social change and may ultimately push society into a new equilibrium.

21 Nancy, a dean at a political institution.

22 Women are 50 percent more likely to be hired by an institution in crisis—this phenomenon has been termed the glass cliff. Institutional leaders realize they need something different to succeed and hiring a woman is visually opposite from the male predecessor. However, being hired into impossible situations often sets women up for failure. Women are then blamed for leadership failure and dismissed. The glass cliff may be a contributing factor for the stagnating numbers of women in leadership positions. See Max Reinwald, Johannes Zaia, and Florian Kunze, "Shine Bright Like a Diamond: When Signaling Creates Glass Cliffs for Female

Executives," *Journal of Management* 49, no. 3 (March 1, 2023): 1005–1036, https://doi.org/10.1177/01492063211067518.

23 Out of the forty-one women interviewed, thirty-nine women had been influenced by a mentor and twenty-five described having had a sponsor. Statistically, only about a third of women have a mentor. See Stephanie Neal, Jazmine Boatman, and Linda Miller, "Women as Mentors: Does She or Doesn't She? A Global Study of Businesswomen and Mentoring," https://www.ddiworld.com/ddi/media/trend-research/womenasmentors_rr_ddi.pdf?ext=.pdf (Development Dimensions International, Inc., 2013), https://www.womensdigitallibrary.org/items/show/121. However, just over 95 percent of these women described having a mentor—significantly above average.

24 Cynthia, a college president at a political institution.

25 Ibarra, Carter, and Silva, "Why Men Still Get More Promotions Than Women." Ibarra et al. highlight sponsorship as the type of mentorship that men receive more than women and as *the* defining reason why women do not advance at the same rate as men.

26 Research has confirmed that sponsorship is the most effective type of mentorship to help both men and women advance. See Taneisha N. Means and Kimberly Fields, "Building and Sustaining an Academic Pipeline by the Sponsorship of Women of Color Political Scientists," *Political Science & Politics* 55, no. 2 (2022): 372–375, https://doi.org/10.1017/S1049096521001803.

27 Ibarra, Carter, and Silva, "Why Men Still Get More Promotions Than Women."

28 Carol S. Dweck, *Mindset: The New Psychology of Success*, updated ed. (New York: Ballantine Books, 2007). Carol Dweck's work on mindset is a simple concept with revolutionary impact. Her differentiation of a fixed mindset from a growth mindset provides a distinction for each of us to consider about the limitations we place on our own capability.

29 Cathy, a dean at an anarchical institution.

30 Dweck, *Mindset*. Passers' growth mindset may have given them capability to grow into something other women had decided was off-limits.

CHAPTER THREE

1 For more information about the waves of feminism, see Abigail Favale, *The Genesis of Gender: A Christian Theory* (San Francisco California: Ignatius Press, 2022); Kimberlé Crenshaw, *Critical Race Theory: The Key Writings That Formed the Movement* (New York: New Press, 1995); "Four

Waves of Feminism," Pacific University, October 25, 2015, https://www.pacificu.edu/magazine/four-waves-feminism; "What Are the Four Waves of Feminism?," History.com, March 11, 2022, https://www.history.com/news/feminism-four-waves.

2 Judith P. Newcombe and Clifton F. Conrad, "A Theory of Mandated Academic Change," *The Journal of Higher Education* 52, no. 6 (1981): 555–577, https://doi.org/10.2307/1981767. This book came out after a season when higher education had experienced significant change (1970s). There are insights into change agents and promoting progress in times of change that have relevance for higher education today, which is yet another season of transition.

3 Newcombe and Conrad, 566.

4 Émile Durkheim first introduced the idea of deviance, reasoning that deviance is an effect of social functions and dysfunctions. According to Durkheim, deviant behavior plays an active, constructive role in society by ultimately helping to cohere different populations within a particular society. "A society probably needs deviants because, as long as some members are considered deviants by the rest of society, attempts to control them set boundaries of acceptable, expected behavior for all other members" (Cuff and Payne, *Perspectives in Sociology*, 60). Thus, deviance is viewed as a way for society to change over time—including positive deviance that leads to positive change. However, deviance may not be recognized as positive until after a new normal has been achieved.

5 These books deal with the antiquated ideal worker model and greedy institutions. Ward and Wolf-Wendel, *Academic Motherhood*; Kelly E. Wilk, "Work-Life Balance and Ideal Worker Expectations for Administrators," *New Directions for Higher Education* 2016, no. 176 (December 1, 2016): 37–51, https://doi.org/10.1002/he.20208; Joan C. Williams, *Reshaping the Work-Family Debate* (Cambridge, MA: Harvard University Press, 2010).

6 Williams, *Reshaping the Work-Family Debate*. This book examines policies in the work-family debate that are "family-hostile policies" held by inflexible workplaces.

7 Working mothers evaluate themselves through the "intensive mothering" and "ideal worker" ideologies, according to Batram-Zantvoort et al. These measuring sticks can increase maternal guilt and decrease women's health. Batram-Zantvoort et al., "Maternal Self-Conception and Mental Wellbeing during the First Wave of the COVID-19 Pandemic."

8 Lewis A. Coser, *Greedy Institutions: Patterns of Undivided Commitment* (New York: Free Press, 1974). Another insight into the significance of

greedy institutions can be found in the book *How Colleges Work* by Robert Birnbaum. Birnbaum offers the helpful analogy of "the black box" with a crank to explain a loosely coupled system in which causes and effects are not clearly linked. When the crank is turned, the gears turn the rotor, but sometimes the gears turn the rotor clockwise and other times turn it counterclockwise. The black box is unpredictable because one cannot see inside the box, so the process of causation, and therefore the outcome, is unpredictable. The loosely coupled university is made up of smaller systems, like gears, that have independent goals that may or may not line up with the goal of the overall system. Similarly, the academic pipeline operates like a black box with loose gears. Women in higher education have competing goals between work and family, and other variables, like lack of sponsorship or deviant behavior, seem to affect the output, that is, women becoming leaders.

9 Moe and Shandy termed the most extreme version of this the "Opt-Out Revolution." Though many women in this study did not completely opt out of advancement, they did not accept every opportunity for promotion because of family pressures and needs.

10 Maureen Baker, "Gendered Families, Academic Work and the 'Motherhood Penalty,'" *Women's Studies Journal* 26, no. 1 (2012): 11–24. This article focuses on "the importance of gendered families, demonstrating that regardless of educational qualifications and occupational prestige, women are more likely than men to fit their employment around their family's needs. They do this out of love, to avoid marital conflict, to 'perform gender', and from lack of alternative support. Furthermore, childfree women are still more likely than mothers with several children to reach the highest academic ranks, and women who reach the senior ranks more often remain single, become separated or divorced, and produce fewer children than they might otherwise have chosen," (22).

11 Birnbaum, *How Colleges Work*. The collegial institution (usually with a small student population) emphasizes collaboration, equal participation, concern for human resources, and the practice of consensus to establish goals and make decisions. Focused primarily on residential, undergraduate education, collegial institutions pursue professors who are teaching-focused and willing to advise students. The bureaucratic institution (typically medium in size) stresses logical decision-making through a formal structure that relies on rules, regulations, hierarchy, and goals. Offering both certifications and undergraduate degrees, bureaucratic institutions attract commuter, part-time, and nontraditional students.

12 Adrienne, a president of a collegial institution.
13 Anna, a president of a bureaucratic institution.
14 Talcott Parsons, *The Social System* (Glencoe, IL: Free Press, 1951).
15 Durkheim, *The Division of Labor in Society*.
16 Cuff and Payne, *Perspectives in Sociology*.
17 Sociologist Gosta Esping-Andersen believes the current situation is an *incomplete revolution*, which he describes as women's life course becoming increasingly masculinized and leading to disequilibria in family. Despite significant shifts for women, cultural norms have not yet caught up—equilibrium has not been achieved. The ramifications of this disequilibrium include that the actions of women in the workplace and even more as leaders is viewed as behavior that deviates from social norms and expectations. When behavior is viewed as deviant by members of society, fewer people act in this way because people innately desire affirmation and approval. Although deviance can change culture, potential leaders need development and support.

CHAPTER FOUR

1 Robert Jervis, *Perception and Misperception in International Politics* (Princeton, NJ: Princeton University Press, 1976).
2 Birnbaum, *How Colleges Work*. In a characteristically large, political institution, organizational structure forms around competition for resources and the varied interests of individuals and groups within the institution. Political institutions are more likely to emphasize research—evidenced by graduate degree programs and the expectations of the faculty. The anarchical institution, usually with an extra-large student body, focuses on the role of symbols (stories, traditions, rituals) in creating meaning for those within the institution. Ethnically, religiously, and politically diverse, anarchical institutions offer the widest range of degrees from undergraduate, graduate, and professional studies.
3 Corneliu Bjola, "Diplomatic Leadership in Times of International Crisis: The Maverick, the Congregator and the Pragmatist," *The Hague Journal of Diplomacy* 10, no. 1 (January 27, 2015): 8, https://doi.org/10.1163/18 71191X-12341300.
4 Bjola, "Diplomatic Leadership in Times of International Crisis."
5 Coser, *Greedy Institutions*. The idea of greedy institutions resurfaces with the conversation about the demands of children, particularly in the younger years.

6 Barbara Cozza and Ceceilia Parnther, eds., *Voices from Women Leaders on Success in Higher Education: Pipelines, Pathways, and Promotion* (New York: Routledge, 2022).
7 Ruchika Tulshyan and Jodi-Ann Burey, "Stop Telling Women They Have Imposter Syndrome," *Harvard Business Review*, February 11, 2021, https://hbr.org/2021/02/stop-telling-women-they-have-imposter-syndrome. This is a well-written, spunky response to the outbreak of imposter syndrome.
8 Tulshyan and Burey. These two have identified the structural errors in imposter syndrome, explaining how it puts "the blame on individuals, without accounting for the historical and cultural contexts that are foundational to how it manifests in both women of color and white women. Imposter syndrome directs our view toward fixing women at work instead of fixing the places where women work." Whew! Good news, women, we do not have to take on the identity of imposters! Rather, this article suggests we join in creating supportive and encouraging work cultures where we can both fail and succeed while we learn and grow together.
9 Jones, *Women Who Opt Out*. I borrow this "opting out" language because it succinctly describes the fullness of the situation in which a qualified woman asserts agency to step back or down the ladder.
10 Mark S. Granovetter, "The Strength of Weak Ties," *American Journal of Sociology* 78, no. 6 (1973): 1360–1380. Granovetter flips the tables on traditional notions of networking or being well-connected. Weak ties, Granovetter says, provide the "diffusion of influence and information, mobility opportunity, and community organization" (1360).

CHAPTER FIVE

1 Institutional type is the main part of the context. To classify the institutions included in this study, I borrowed Birnbaum's typology from *How College Works* (1988). These four types (collegial, bureaucratic, political, and anarchical) have been referenced and explained throughout the book.
2 I imagine this concept could be perceived differently than I intend. You may be thinking that constraints are not gifts but real problems that need to be addressed. You would be correct. However, what I mean to say is that rather than feeling like a victim of the constraint, women with responsive agency reframe the constraint to their own advantage. In other words, as the English proverb states, "necessity is the mother of invention." Without the constraint, there is no need for an innovative response.

3 Bees are not the enemies, although they can be volatile. When they feel threatened, they can use their sting to protect themselves, but the primary purpose of bees is not to harm. Bees productively cross-pollinate plants and make honey. Bees are necessary to the flourishing of the garden. Diversity in the garden allows for growth. Diversity also benefits humanity.

4 These sources reinforce that women continue to carry the majority of the domestic load. Heggeness and Fields, "Working Moms Bear Brunt of Home Schooling While Working During COVID-19"; Lyn Craig and Brendan Churchill, "Working and Caring at Home: Gender Differences in the Effects of Covid-19 on Paid and Unpaid Labor in Australia," *Feminist Economics* 27, no. 1–2 (April 3, 2021): 310–326, https://doi.org/10.1080/13545701.2020.1831039; Hayes and Lee, "Women, Work, and Families during the COVID-19 Pandemic"; Petts, Carlson, and Pepin, "A Gendered Pandemic"; Hochschild and Machung, *The Second Shift*; Crittenden, *The Price of Motherhood*; Ulf Ericsson et al., "Work, Family Life and Recovery: An Exploratory Study of 'the Third Shift,'" *Work* 70, no. 4 (2021): 1131–1140, https://doi.org/10.3233/WOR-213624.

5 Arthur Yeung and Dave Ulrich, *Reinventing the Organization: How Companies Can Deliver Radically Greater Value in Fast-Changing Markets* (La Vergne, TN: Harvard Business Review Press, 2019). Organizational behavior theory helps us understand the systemic dynamics that must be navigated. The concept of *responsiveness* in organizational behavior reveals the importance of accounting for the unique environment of the organization.

6 The Old Testament historical narrative of Ruth and Naomi illustrates the persuasive and spiritual power of women to reframe a bleak situation. Ruth, a young widow, needed a husband and her mother-in-law, Naomi knew Boaz could offer the familial covering Ruth needed. Naomi's inventive plan for Ruth to hide until night and to uncover Boaz's feet seemed unconventional at best. Yet, Ruth effectively hid herself, blending in until jumping into action to convey her intent. Ruth garnered Boaz's attention with her symbolic act and, ultimately, he gifted her the covering of his protection, fulfilling the duty of kinsman-redeemer. However, success was born through Naomi's creativity. At first, this example may portray an antiquated undervaluing of the role of women. Admittedly, women at that time and in that society were reliant on marriage for financial provision, yet Naomi and Ruth did not begin by trying to change the structure or even the culture. Instead, they worked innovatively within those bounds to achieve the provision of their basic needs. Additionally, their cultural

circumstances shifted enormously from being lowly widows to being a part of Boaz's wealthy estate—a remarkable increase in status. Naomi and Ruth creatively found a way forward that deviated from cultural norms, but it certainly was not the only way forward. Women have acted with conscious responsiveness from ancient times to modern days and throughout the centuries sandwiched in between.

7 Tanja Hentschel, Madeline E. Heilman, and Claudia V. Peus, "The Multiple Dimensions of Gender Stereotypes: A Current Look at Men's and Women's Characterizations of Others and Themselves," *Frontiers in Psychology* 10 (2019), https://www.frontiersin.org/articles/10.3389/fpsyg.2019.00011. Even though we are working toward equality culturally, women and men do not characterize themselves equally. This study found that gender stereotypes persist within the minds of many women and men. One relevant finding was that females rated themselves as less agentic than males.

8 Eileen M. Collins and Jonathan H. Ward, *Through the Glass Ceiling to the Stars: The Story of the First American Woman to Command a Space Mission* (New York: Arcade, 2021), 18. If you want to be inspired, buy this book and read it immediately. I read much of this memoir aloud to my seven-year-old daughter, and we both found it intriguing and hard to put down. Eileen is relatable and her story compelling. She shares the hardships of navigating family and work while pursuing her lifelong dream.

9 Nick Brancazio, "Gender and the Senses of Agency," *Phenomenology and the Cognitive Sciences* 18, no. 2 (April 1, 2019): 425–440, https://doi.org/10.1007/s11097-018-9581-z. I appreciate Brancazio's approach. Rather than focusing solely on the cognitive gender structures, Brancazio seeks to evaluate the embodied gender structures. His insights confirm that action and cognition work together to shape our reality.

10 "What Is Compound Growth—Wells Fargo," accessed April 17, 2023, https://www.wellsfargo.com/financial-education/investing/compound-interest-growth/. Read more about investing basics and how to get compound growth to work for you.

11 Eugen H. Peterson, *The Message Bible*, Deluxe, Gift ed. (NavPress, 2019). Proverbs 12:24. "The diligent find freedom in their work; the lazy are oppressed by work." *The Message* translation of the Bible puts ancient biblical text into everyday language.

12 Shaun Gallagher, "Philosophical Conceptions of the Self: Implications for Cognitive Science," *Trends in Cognitive Sciences* 4, no. 1 (January 2000): 14–21, https://doi.org/10.1016/S1364-6613(99)01417-5. Gallagher explains two concepts of self: the minimal self and the narrative self. This distinction is complex and significant for our understanding of agency.

13 Brancazio, "Gender and the Senses of Agency," 428. Brancazio brings microscopic clarity to the woman as agent of her life.
14 Kimberlé Crenshaw, "Mapping the Margins: Intersectionality, Identity Politics, and Violence against Women of Color," *Stanford Law Review* 43, no. 6 (1991): 1241–1299, https://doi.org/10.2307/1229039. Crenshaw's works are foundational reads on the subject of intersectionality.
15 Crenshaw, "Mapping the Margins," 1241. Intersectional identity beautifully moves the identity discussion from one-dimensional to multi-dimensional—a fuller and more accurate description of a woman's reality.
16 A few of the women academic leaders did not have children, but many of those had other identities, such as being a racial minority.
17 Favale, *The Genesis of Gender*. Favale delicately deals with the subject of gender through the biblical lens of Genesis.
18 Willie James Jennings, *The Christian Imagination, Theology and the Origins of Race* (Yale University Press, 2010), https://www.jstor.org/stable/j.ctt1np8j2.11. "To change one's way of imagining connection and one's way of desiring joining is no small thing. Yet I am convinced that such a change is not only necessary but now stands before human communities as the only real option for survival in a world of dwindling natural resources and tightening global economic chains of commodification. To imagine along the direction I suggest . . . would be nothing less than a theological act, indeed, a Christian act of imagining. And if, as I believe, Christian life is indeed a way forward for the world, then it must reemerge as a compelling new invitation to life together," 294.
19 Zora Neale Hurston, *Their Eyes Were Watching God*, rev. ed. (New York: Amistad, 2006).
20 Hurston beautifully captures the social expectations and actions of women on the first page of the book: "Now, women forget all those things they don't want to remember and remember everything they don't want to forget. The dream is the truth. Then they act and do things accordingly." Hurston, *Their Eyes Were Watching God*, 1.
21 Laura L. Koppes Bryan, *Shaping Work-Life Culture in Higher Education: A Guide for Academic Leaders* (New York: Routledge, Taylor & Francis Group, 2015); Ibarra, Ely, and Kolb, "Women Rising"; Sheryl Sandberg, *Lean in: Women, Work, and the Will to Lead* (New York: Alfred A. Knopf, 2013); "Barriers and Bias."
22 A nod to a friend, pastor, and great thinker, Mick R. Murray, and some of his thoughts that influenced mine.
23 Emilie M. Townes, "Everydayness: Beginning Notes on Dismantling the Cultural Production of Evil," in *Womanist Ethics and the Cultural*

Production of Evil, ed. Emilie M. Townes, Black Religion / Womanist Thought / Social Justice (New York: Palgrave Macmillan US, 2006), 159, https://doi.org/10.1057/9780230601628_8. Townes has a penetrating style and is able to engage difficult topics with both assertiveness and kindness at a deeply personal level.

24 Mustafa Emirbayer and Ann Mische, "What Is Agency?," *American Journal of Sociology* 103, no. 4 (1998): 962–1023, https://doi.org/10.1086/231294. Tracing the historical understanding of agency, Emirbayer and Mische provide a helpful timeline from a sociological perspective while cutting through the ambiguity and vagueness of the topic itself.

25 Emirbayer and Mische, "What Is Agency?"

26 Townes suggests this "ancient" vision of justice and peace—evoking a biblical directive.

27 E. J. Lowe, *Personal Agency: The Metaphysics of Mind and Action* (Oxford: University Press, 2008), 199. Lowe is a deep thinker, and his understanding of the self far surpasses my limited understanding. Yet, his writing encourages my belief that responsive agency is indeed available.

28 Emirbayer and Mische, "What Is Agency?"

29 Colin Campbell, "Distinguishing the Power of Agency from Agentic Power: A Note on Weber and the 'Black Box' of Personal Agency," *Sociological Theory* 27, no. 4 (2009): 407–418, https://doi.org/10.1111/j.1467-9558.2009.01355.x. Campbell attempts to demystify the concept of agency. His contribution is separating the power of agency from agentic power and finding that you need both.

30 The Psalmist says that we were created with intention. "For you formed my inward parts; you knitted me together in my mother's womb. I praise you, for I am fearfully and wonderfully made. Wonderful are your works; my soul knows it very well." Psalm 139:13–14, English Standard Version (ESV).

31 Sharon L. Harlan and Catherine White Berheide, "Barriers to Work Place Advancement Experienced by Women in Low-Paying Occupations" (Washington DC: U.S. Glass Ceiling Commission, 1994); Carol Hymowitz, "Through the Glass Ceiling," *Wall Street Journal*, November 9, 2004, sec. Special, http://www.wsj.com/articles/SB109959142722364961; Ibarra and Ely, "Educate Everyone About Second-Generation Gender Bias"; Jones, *Women Who Opt Out*; Moe and Shandy, *Glass Ceilings and 100-Hour Couples*.

32 Paula J. Caplan, "Why Can't a Woman Be More Like a Man?, or The Maleness of the Environment," in *Lifting a Ton of Feathers, A Woman's Guide to Surviving in the Academic World* (University of Toronto Press,

1993), 26–33, http://www.jstor.org/stable/10.3138/j.ctt1287rwj.6. Caplan considers the limitations of gender roles in the academy and the struggle women face trying to conform to (or bypass) conventional expectations.

33 American Council on Education, "Moving the Needle," Media Kit, 2016, http://www.acenet.edu/about-ace/special-initiatives/Pages/Moving-the-Needle-Together.aspx. The "Moving the Needle" initiative was one of the first I encountered when I began my research on women leaders in higher education. This is a motivated and committed group, which began in 2010 and seeks gender parity within the academy.

34 Bruno Broucker et al., *Transformation Fast and Slow: Digitalisation, Quality and Trust in Higher Education*, vol. 3, Higher Education: Linking Research, Policy and Practice (Leiden: Brill, 2022). This is a highly relevant book on how the COVID-19 pandemic transformed higher education.

35 Research demands are shifting the focus and landscape of the university. This will undoubtedly affect women's path to leadership. "Business Research Makes up a Majority of Penn's Non-Science and Engineering Research Expenditures," accessed June 7, 2023, https://datawrapper.dwcdn.net/Lj9eg/1/; "UTSA Research Expenditures at an All-Time High for Third Year in a Row," January 4, 2023, https://www.utsa.edu/today/2023/01/story/fy22-research-expenditures-at-all-time-high.html.

36 Of course, this way of living requires courage, which is not an intellectual act; rather, it is an act of the will.

BIBLIOGRAPHY

AAUW: Empowering Women Since 1881. "Barriers and Bias: The Status of Women in Leadership," March 2016. http://www.aauw.org/research/barriers-and-bias/.

Allen, Tammy D., Rachel Day, and Elizabeth Lentz. "The Role of Interpersonal Comfort in Mentoring Relationships." *Journal of Career Development* 31, no. 3 (2005): 155–169.

American Council on Education. "ACE Convenes Discussion on Women in Higher Education." *Gender Equity* (blog), July 16, 2012. http://www.acenet.edu/news-room/Pages/Discussion-Women-Leadership.aspx.

———. "American College President Study." American Council on Education, 2017. http://www.acenet.edu/news-room/Pages/American-College-President-Study.aspx.

———. "Moving the Needle." Media Kit, 2016. http://www.acenet.edu/about-ace/special-initiatives/Pages/Moving-the-Needle-Together.aspx.

Baker, Maureen. "Gendered Families, Academic Work and the 'Motherhood Penalty.'" *Women's Studies Journal* 26, no. 1 (2012): 11–24.

Batram-Zantvoort, Stephanie, Lisa Wandschneider, Vera Niehues, Oliver Razum, and Céline Miani. "Maternal Self-Conception and Mental Wellbeing during the First Wave of the COVID-19 Pandemic." *Frontiers in Global Women's Health* 3 (2022). https://www.frontiersin.org/articles/10.3389/fgwh.2022.878723.

Belkin, Lisa. "The Opt-Out Revolution." *New York Times*, October 26, 2003, sec. Magazine. https://www.nytimes.com/2003/10/26/magazine/the-opt-out-revolution.html.

Bianchi, Suzanne M., Liana C. Sayer, Melissa A. Milkie, and John P. Robinson. "Housework: Who Did, Does or Will Do It, and How Much Does It Matter?" *Social Forces: A Scientific Medium of Social Study and Interpretation* 91, no. 1 (September 1, 2012): 55–63. https://doi.org/10.1093/sf/sos120.

Birnbaum, Robert. *How Colleges Work: The Cybernetics of Academic Organization and Leadership*. Wiley, 1991.

Bjola, Corneliu. "Diplomatic Leadership in Times of International Crisis: The Maverick, the Congregator and the Pragmatist." *The Hague Journal of Diplomacy* 10, no. 1 (January 27, 2015): 4–9. https://doi.org/10.1163/1871191X-12341300.

Brancazio, Nick. "Gender and the Senses of Agency." *Phenomenology and the Cognitive Sciences* 18, no. 2 (April 1, 2019): 425–440. https://doi.org/10.1007/s11097-018-9581-z.

Bras, Hilde, Aart C. Liefbroer, and Cees H. Elzinga. "Standardization of Pathways to Adulthood? An Analysis of Dutch Cohorts Born Between 1850 and 1900." *Demography* 47, no. 4 (November 2010): 1013–1034.

Braun, Hillary J. "How Should We Address the Pipeline Problem?" *Perspectives on Medical Education* 5, no. 2 (April 2016): 75–77. https://doi.org/10.1007/s40037-016-0266-4.

Brewer, Ann M. *Mentoring from a Positive Psychology Perspective: Learning for Mentors and Mentees*. Springer, 2016.

Broucker, Bruno, Rosalind M. O. Pritchard, Clare Milsom, René Krempkow, and ProQuest. *Transformation Fast and Slow: Digitalisation, Quality and Trust in Higher Education*. Vol. 3. Higher Education: Linking Research, Policy and Practice. Leiden: Brill, 2022.

Bryan, Laura L. Koppes. *Shaping Work-Life Culture in Higher Education: A Guide for Academic Leaders*. New York: Routledge, Taylor & Francis Group, 2015.

"Business Research Makes up a Majority of Penn's Non-Science and Engineering Research Expenditures." Accessed June 7, 2023. https://datawrapper.dwcdn.net/Lj9eg/1/.

Campbell, Colin. "Distinguishing the Power of Agency from Agentic Power: A Note on Weber and the 'Black Box' of Personal Agency." *Sociological Theory* 27, no. 4 (2009): 407–418. https://doi.org/10.1111/j.1467-9558.2009.01355.x.

Caplan, Paula J. "Why Can't a Woman Be More Like a Man?, or The Maleness of the Environment." In *Lifting a Ton of Feathers: A Woman's Guide to Surviving in the Academic World*, 26–33. University of Toronto Press, 1993. http://www.jstor.org/stable/10.3138/j.ctt1287rwj.6.

Cardozo, Arlene Rossen. *Sequencing*. New York: Collier Books, 1989.

Carli, Linda L., and Alice H. Eagly. "Women Face a Labyrinth: An Examination of Metaphors for Women Leaders." *Gender in Management: An International Journal* 31, no. 8 (October 27, 2016): 514–527. https://doi.org/10.1108/GM-02-2015-0007.

Carnevale, Anthony P., Nicole Smith, and Artem Gulish. "Women Can't Win: Despite Making Educational Gains and Pursuing High Wage Majors,

Women Still Earn Less Than Men." Georgetown University Center on Education and the Workforce, 2018. https://cew.georgetown.edu/cew-reports/genderwagegap/.

Catalyst. "Women CEOs of the S&P 500 Companies." Text. Catalyst, August 2017. http://www.catalyst.org/knowledge/women-ceos-sp-500.

Chao, Georgia T., Pat M. Walz, and Philip D. Gardner. "Formal and Informal Mentorships: A Comparison on Mentoring Functions and Contrast with Nonmentored Counterparts." *Personnel Psychology; Durham* 45, no. 3 (Autumn 1992): 619.

Cohn, Samuel. *Race, Gender, and Discrimination at Work*. Boulder, CO: Westview Press, 2009.

Collins, Eileen M., and Jonathan H. Ward. *Through the Glass Ceiling to the Stars: The Story of the First American Woman to Command a Space Mission*. New York: Arcade, 2021.

Cook, Alison, and Christy Glass. "Above the Glass Ceiling: When Are Women and Racial/Ethnic Minorities Promoted to CEO?" *Strategic Management Journal* 35, no. 7 (July 1, 2014): 1080–1089. https://doi.org/10.1002/smj.2161.

Coser, Lewis A. *Greedy Institutions: Patterns of Undivided Commitment*. New York: Free Press, 1974.

Cox, Kelline Sue. "Motivational Factors Influencing Women's Decisions to Pursue Upper-Level Administrative Positions in Higher Education." PhD diss., Kansas State University, 2008.

Cozza, Barbara, and Ceceilia Parnther, eds. *Voices from Women Leaders on Success in Higher Education: Pipelines, Pathways, and Promotion*. New York: Routledge, 2022.

Craig, Lyn, and Brendan Churchill. "Working and Caring at Home: Gender Differences in the Effects of Covid-19 on Paid and Unpaid Labor in Australia." *Feminist Economics* 27, no. 1–2 (April 3, 2021): 310–326. https://doi.org/10.1080/13545701.2020.1831039.

Crenshaw, Kimberlé. *Critical Race Theory: The Key Writings That Formed the Movement*. New York: New Press, 1995.

———. "Mapping the Margins: Intersectionality, Identity Politics, and Violence against Women of Color." *Stanford Law Review* 43, no. 6 (1991): 1241–1299. https://doi.org/10.2307/1229039.

Creswell, Julie. "Even After the Glass Ceiling Yields, Female Executives Find Shaky Ground." *New York Times*, August 3, 2017, sec. Business Day. https://www.nytimes.com/2017/08/03/business/female-ceos-glass-cliff.html.

Crittenden, Ann. *The Price of Motherhood: Why the Most Important Job in the World Is Still the Least Valued*. 10th anniversary edition. New York: Picador, 2010.

Cuff, E. C., and G. C. F. Payne, eds. *Perspectives in Sociology*. 2nd ed. London; Boston: Allen & Unwin, 1984.

Dawkins, Marcia Alesan. *Clearly Invisible: Racial Passing and the Color of Cultural Identity*. Waco, TX: Baylor University Press, 2012.

DeRue, D. Scott, and Susan J. Ashford. "Who Will Lead and Who Will Follow? A Social Process of Leadership Identity Construction in Organizations." *Academy of Management Review* 35, no. 4 (October 2010): 627–647.

Durkheim, Émile. *The Division of Labor in Society*. Translated by W. D. Halls. New York: Free Press, 1912.

Dweck, Carol S. *Mindset: The New Psychology of Success*. Updated ed. New York: Ballantine Books, 2007.

Eagly, Alice Hendrickson, and Linda Lorene Carli. *Through the Labyrinth: The Truth about How Women Become Leaders*. Boston, MA: Harvard Business School Press, 2007.

Emirbayer, Mustafa, and Ann Mische. "What Is Agency?" *American Journal of Sociology* 103, no. 4 (1998): 962–1023. https://doi.org/10.1086/231294.

Ericsson, Ulf, Pär Pettersson, Leif W. Rydstedt, and Elin Ekelund. "Work, Family Life and Recovery: An Exploratory Study of 'the Third Shift.'" *Work* 70, no. 4 (2021): 1131–1140. https://doi.org/10.3233/WOR-213624.

Esping-Andersen, Gosta. *Incomplete Revolution: Adapting Welfare States to Women's New Roles*. Cambridge: Polity Press, 2009.

Fagenson-Eland, Ellen A. "Perceptions of Mentoring Relationships." *Journal of Vocational Behavior* 51, no. 1 (1997): 29–42.

Farnham, Christie, ed. *Women of the American South: A Multicultural Reader*. New York: New York University Press, 1997.

Favale, Abigail. *The Genesis of Gender: A Christian Theory*. San Francisco California: Ignatius Press, 2022.

"Four Waves of Feminism." Pacific University. October 25, 2015. https://www.pacificu.edu/magazine/four-waves-feminism.

Friday, Yolanda Cleveland. "The Impact of Mentorship and Sponsorship on the Job Satisfaction of Female Student Affairs Administrators." PhD diss., The Claremont Graduate University, 2014. https://search-proquest-com.ezproxy.baylor.edu/pqdtglobal/docview/1527107887/abstract/271CD1602C6A4350PQ/1.

Gallagher, Shaun. "Philosophical Conceptions of the Self: Implications for Cognitive Science." *Trends in Cognitive Sciences* 4, no. 1 (January 2000): 14–21. https://doi.org/10.1016/S1364-6613(99)01417-5.

García-Manglano, Javier, Natalia Nollenberger, and Almudena Sevilla. "Gender, Time-Use, and Fertility Recovery in Industrialized Countries." In *International Encyclopedia of the Social & Behavioral Sciences*, 775–80, 2015. https://doi.org/10.1016/B978-0-08-097086-8.31104-7.

Goffman, Erving. *Stigma: Notes on the Management of Spoiled Identity*. Spectrum Book. Englewood Cliffs, NJ: Prentice-Hall, 1963.

Goldin, Claudia. "The Quiet Revolution That Transformed Women's Employment, Education, and Family." Working Paper. National Bureau of Economic Research, January 2006. https://doi.org/10.3386/w11953.

Granovetter, Mark S. "The Strength of Weak Ties." *American Journal of Sociology* 78, no. 6 (1973): 1360–1380.

Guess, Teresa J. "The Social Construction of Whiteness: Racism by Intent, Racism by Consequence." *Critical Sociology* 32, no. 4 (July 1, 2006): 649–673. https://doi.org/10.1163/156916306779155199.

Harlan, Sharon L., and Catherine White Berheide. "Barriers to Work Place Advancement Experienced by Women in Low-Paying Occupations." Washington DC: U.S. Glass Ceiling Commission, 1994.

Hayes, Amy Roberson, and Diamond Lee. "Women, Work, and Families during the COVID-19 Pandemic: Examining the Effects of COVID Policies and Looking to the Future." *Journal of Social Issues* 79, no. 3 (June 2022): 1088–1105. https://doi.org/10.1111/josi.12510.

Hazelkorn, Ellen. *Rankings and the Reshaping of Higher Education: The Battle for World-Class Excellence*. Basingstoke, Hampshire, GBR: Palgrave Macmillan, 2011.

Heggeness, Misty L., and Jason M. Fields. "Working Moms Bear Brunt of Home Schooling While Working During COVID-19." Census.gov, August 18, 2020. https://www.census.gov/library/stories/2020/08/parents-juggle-work-and-child-care-during-pandemic.html.

Henderson, Tim. "Mothers Are 3 Times More Likely Than Fathers to Have Lost Jobs in Pandemic." News. Stateline, September 28, 2020. https://stateline.org/2020/09/28/mothers-are-3-times-more-likely-than-fathers-to-have-lost-jobs-in-pandemic/.

Hentschel, Tanja, Madeline E. Heilman, and Claudia V. Peus. "The Multiple Dimensions of Gender Stereotypes: A Current Look at Men's and Women's Characterizations of Others and Themselves." *Frontiers in Psychology* 10 (2019). https://www.frontiersin.org/articles/10.3389/fpsyg.2019.00011.

Hewlett, Sylvia Ann, Kerrie Peraino, Laura Sherbin, and Karen Sumberg. "The Sponsor Effect: Breaking through the Last Glass Ceiling." Boston, MA: Harvard Business School Publishing, December 2010.

Hinchlife, Emma. "Women Run More than 10% of Fortune 500 Companies for the First Time." *Fortune*, January 12, 2023. https://fortune.com/2023/01/12/fortune-500-companies-ceos-women-10-percent/.

Hochschild, Arlie. *The Second Shift: Working Parents and the Revolution at Home*. New York: Viking, 1989.

Hochschild, Arlie, and Anne Machung. *The Second Shift: Working Families and the Revolution at Home*. Rev. ed. New York: Penguin Books, 2012.

Hurston, Zora Neale. *Their Eyes Were Watching God*. Rev. ed. New York: Amistad, 2006.

Hussar, Bill, Jijun Zhang, Sarah Hein, Ke Wang, Ashley Roberts, Jiashan Cui, Mary Smith, Farrah Bullock Mann, Amy Barmer, and Rita Dilig. "The Condition of Education 2020. NCES 2020–144." National Center for Education Statistics, May 2020. https://eric.ed.gov/?id=ED605216.

Hymowitz, Carol. "Through the Glass Ceiling." *Wall Street Journal*, November 9, 2004, sec. Special. http://www.wsj.com/articles/SB109959142722364961.

Ibarra, Herminia, Nancy M. Carter, and Christine Silva. "Why Men Still Get More Promotions Than Women." *Harvard Business Review*, September 1, 2010. https://hbr.org/2010/09/why-men-still-get-more-promotions-than-women.

Ibarra, Herminia, and Robin J. Ely. "Educate Everyone About Second-Generation Gender Bias." *Harvard Business Review*, August 21, 2013. https://hbr.org/2013/08/educate-everyone-about-second.

Ibarra, Herminia, Robin J. Ely, and Deborah M. Kolb. "Women Rising: The Unseen Barriers." *Harvard Business Review*, September 1, 2013. https://hbr.org/2013/09/women-rising-the-unseen-barriers.

Jennings, Willie James. *The Christian Imagination: Theology and the Origins of Race*. Yale University Press, 2010. https://www.jstor.org/stable/j.ctt1np8j2.11.

Jervis, Robert. *Perception and Misperception in International Politics*. Princeton, NJ: Princeton University Press, 1976.

Jinyoung Hwang, and Jong Ha Lee. "Women's Education and the Timing and Level of Fertility." *International Journal of Social Economics* 41, no. 9 (August 19, 2014): 862–874. https://doi.org/10.1108/IJSE-06-2013-0153.

Jones, Bernie D., ed. *Women Who Opt Out: The Debate over Working Mothers and Work-Family Balance*. NYU Press, 2012. http://www.jstor.org/stable/j.ctt9qg9pg.

Kangas, Nicole Lynn. "Forming Families and Careers: The Effects of Family Size, First Birth Timing, and Early Family Aspirations on U.S. Women's Mental Health, Labor Force Participation, and Career Choices." PhD diss., Stanford University, 2011.

Kimmel, Michael S., and Amy B. Aronson. *Men and Masculinities: A Social, Cultural, and Historical Encyclopedia.* ABC-CLIO, 2003.

Kleinepier, Tom, and Helga A. G. de Valk. "Ethnic Differences in Family Trajectories of Young Adult Women in the Netherlands: Timing and Sequencing of Events." *Demographic Research; Rostock* 35 (December 2016): 671–710.

Koelet, Suzana, Helga de Valk, Ignace Glorieux, Ilse Laurijssen, and Didier Willaert. "The Timing of Family Commitments in the Early Work Career: Work-Family Trajectories of Young Adults in Flanders." *Demographic Research; Rostock* 32 (June 2015): 657–690.

Kolb, Deborah M. "Negotiating in the Shadows of Organizations: Gender, Negotiation, and Change." *Ohio State Journal on Dispute Resolution* 28, no. 2 (June 2013): 241–262.

Kram, K. E. *Mentoring at Work: Developmental Relationships in Organizational Life.* Glenview, IL: Scott, Foresman, 1985.

Lowe, E. J. *Personal Agency: The Metaphysics of Mind and Action.* Oxford University Press, 2008.

Mason, Mary Ann, Nicholas H. Wolfinger, and Marc Goulden. *Do Babies Matter? Gender and Family in the Ivory Tower.* New Brunswick, NJ: Rutgers University Press, 2013.

McKinsey & Company. "COVID-19's Impact on Women's Employment," March 8, 2021. https://www.mckinsey.com/featured-insights/diversity-and-inclusion/seven-charts-that-show-covid-19s-impact-on-womens-employment.

Means, Taneisha N., and Kimberly Fields. "Building and Sustaining an Academic Pipeline by the Sponsorship of Women of Color Political Scientists." *Political Science & Politics* 55, no. 2 (2022): 372–375. https://doi.org/10.1017/S1049096521001803.

Moe, Karine, and Dianna Shandy, eds. *Glass Ceilings and 100-Hour Couples: What the Opt-Out Phenomenon Can Teach Us about Work and Family.* Athens: University of Georgia Press, 2010.

Nattinger, Ann B. "Promoting the Career Development of Women in Academic Medicine." *Archives of Internal Medicine* 167, no. 4 (February 26, 2007): 323–324. https://doi.org/10.1001/archinte.167.4.323.

Neal, Stephanie, Jazmine Boatman, and Linda Miller. "Women as Mentors: Does She or Doesn't She? A Global Study of Businesswomen and Mentoring." https://www.ddiworld.com/ddi/media/trend-research/

womenasmentors_rr_ddi.pdf?ext=.pdf. Development Dimensions International, Inc., 2013. https://www.womensdigitallibrary.org/items/show/121.

Newcombe, Judith P., and Clifton F. Conrad. "A Theory of Mandated Academic Change." *The Journal of Higher Education* 52, no. 6 (1981): 555–577. https://doi.org/10.2307/1981767.

Noe, Raymond A. "An Investigation of the Determinants of Successful Assigned Mentoring Relationships." *Personnel Psychology* 41, no. 3 (1988): 457–479.

Noe, Raymond A., David B. Greenberger, and Sheng Wang. "Mentoring: What We Know and Where We Might Go." In *Research in Personnel and Human Resources Management*, 21:129–173. Leeds: Emerald Group Publishing Limited, 2002. https://doi.org/10.1016/S0742-7301(02)21003-8.

Parkes, Mrs. William. *Domestic Duties; or, Instructions to Young Married Ladies*. New York: J. & J. Harper, 1829.

Parsons, Talcott. *The Social System*. Glencoe, IL: Free Press, 1951.

Paulus, Jessica K., Karen M. Switkowski, Geneve M. Allison, Molly Connors, Rachel J. Buchsbaum, Karen M. Freund, and Deborah Blazey-Martin. "Where Is the Leak in the Pipeline? Investigating Gender Differences in Academic Promotion at an Academic Medical Centre." *Perspectives on Medical Education* 5, no. 2 (April 2016): 125–128. https://doi.org/10.1007/s40037-016-0263-7.

Peterson, Eugene H. *The Message Bible*. Deluxe, gift edition. NavPress, 2019.

Petts, Richard J., Daniel L. Carlson, and Joanna R. Pepin. "A Gendered Pandemic: Childcare, Homeschooling, and Parents' Employment during COVID-19." *Gender, Work & Organization* 28, no. S2 (2021): 515–534. https://doi.org/10.1111/gwao.12614.

"Pipelines, Pathways, and Institutional Leadership: An Update on the Status of Women in Higher Education." American Council on Education, 2016. http://www.acenet.edu/news-room/Documents/Higher-Ed-Spotlight-Pipelines-Pathways-and-Institutional-Leadership-Status-of-Women.pdf.

Power, Kate. "The COVID-19 Pandemic Has Increased the Care Burden of Women and Families." *Sustainability: Science, Practice and Policy* 16, no. 1 (December 10, 2020): 67–73. https://doi.org/10.1080/15487733.2020.1776561.

Prime, Jeanine, Nancy M. Carter, and Theresa M. Welbourne. "Women 'Take Care,' Men 'Take Charge': Managers' Stereotypic Perceptions of Women and Men Leaders," *The Psychologist-Manager Journal* 12, no.1 (January 2009): 25–49. https://doi.org/10.1080/10887150802371799.

Bibliography

Reinwald, Max, Johannes Zaia, and Florian Kunze. "Shine Bright Like a Diamond: When Signaling Creates Glass Cliffs for Female Executives." *Journal of Management* 49, no. 3 (March 1, 2023): 1005–1036. https://doi.org/10.1177/01492063211067518.

Ryan, Michelle K., and S. Alexander Haslam. "The Glass Cliff: Evidence That Women Are Over-Represented in Precarious Leadership Positions." *British Journal of Management* 16, no. 2 (June 1, 2005): 81–90. https://doi.org/10.1111/j.1467-8551.2005.00433.x.

Sandberg, Sheryl. *Lean in: Women, Work, and the Will to Lead*. New York: Alfred A. Knopf, 2013.

Savage, Hallie E., Rashelle S. Karp, and Rose Logue. "Faculty Mentorship at Colleges and Universities." *College Teaching* 52, no. 1 (2004): 21.

Sexton, Patricia Cayo. *Women in Education*. Perspectives in American Education. Bloomington, IN: Phi Delta Kappa Educational Foundation, 1976.

Shakeshaft, Carol. *Women in Educational Administration*. Updated ed. Newbury Park, CA: Sage Publications, 1989.

Solomon, Barbara Miller. *In the Company of Educated Women: A History of Women and Higher Education in America*. New Haven: Yale University Press, 1985.

Taub, Amanda. "Pandemic Will 'Take Our Women 10 Years Back' in the Workplace." *New York Times*, September 26, 2020, sec. World. https://www.nytimes.com/2020/09/26/world/covid-women-childcare-equality.html.

Thomas, M. E. *Confessions of a Sociopath: A Life Spent Hiding in Plain Sight*. Reprint edition. New York: Crown, 2014.

Townes, Emilie M. "Everydayness: Beginning Notes on Dismantling the Cultural Production of Evil." In *Womanist Ethics and the Cultural Production of Evil*, edited by Emilie M. Townes, 159–165. Black Religion / Womanist Thought / Social Justice. New York: Palgrave Macmillan US, 2006. https://doi.org/10.1057/9780230601628_8.

Tulshyan, Ruchika, and Jodi-Ann Burey. "Stop Telling Women They Have Imposter Syndrome." *Harvard Business Review*, February 11, 2021. https://hbr.org/2021/02/stop-telling-women-they-have-imposter-syndrome.

U.S. Bureau of Labor Statistics. "Current Population Survey," 2015. https://www.bls.gov/cps/cpsaat11.pdf.

U.S. Department of Labor. "Women in the Labor Force." Government. Women in the Labor Force, 2013. https://www.dol.gov/wb/stats/stats_data.htm#mothers.

U.S. Equal Employment Opportunity Commission. "Title VII of the Civil Rights Act of 1964." Government, 1964. https://www.eeoc.gov/laws/statutes/titlevii.cfm.

"UTSA Research Expenditures at an All-Time High for Third Year in a Row," January 4, 2023. https://www.utsa.edu/today/2023/01/story/fy22-research-expenditures-at-all-time-high.html.

Ward, Kelly, and Lisa Wolf-Wendel. *Academic Motherhood: How Faculty Manage Work and Family*. Piscataway: Rutgers University Press, 2012.

"What Are the Four Waves of Feminism?," History.com, March 11, 2022. https://www.history.com/news/feminism-four-waves.

"What Is Compound Growth—Wells Fargo." Accessed April 17, 2023. https://www.wellsfargo.com/financial-education/investing/compound-interest-growth/.

Wilk, Kelly E. "Work-Life Balance and Ideal Worker Expectations for Administrators." *New Directions for Higher Education* 2016, no. 176 (December 1, 2016): 37–51. https://doi.org/10.1002/he.20208.

Williams, Joan C. *Reshaping the Work-Family Debate*. Cambridge, MA: Harvard University Press, 2010.

Wyer, Robert S., and Thomas K. Srull. *Handbook of Social Cognition*. 2nd ed. UK: Psychology Press, 2014.

Yeung, Arthur, and Dave Ulrich. *Reinventing the Organization: How Companies Can Deliver Radically Greater Value in Fast-Changing Markets*. La Vergne, TN: Harvard Business Review Press, 2019.

Zarate, Michael A., and Eliot R. Smith. "Person Categorization and Stereotyping." *Social Cognition; New York* 8, no. 2 (June 1990): 161–185. http://dx.doi.org/10.1521/soco.1990.8.2.161.

INDEX

access, 1–3, 5–6, 11
agency, 38, 69–70, 77–87
   minimal, 80
   narrative, 80–81
Air Force, 80
American Council on Education (ACE), 46

Baby Boomers, 11
Birnbaum, Robert, 91, 114n8
black box, 87, 114n8
burnout, 64

career goals, 6, 26, 52, 81, 82
change agency, 38
childcare, 12, 40, 53, 96
children, 39–42, 51–54, 73, 97n1, 102n19
   mommy guilt, 40, 41
   single parent, 42
   young children, 3, 39, 41, 53–54
clothing, 19, 20
coeducation, 2
collaboration, 55, 56–57, 58–59, 76
Collins, Eileen M., 79–80
community, 29, 39, 58, 69, 74, 86,

community college, 53
compound growth, 80
confidence, xv, 13, 29, 32, 33, 37, 60–6, 71–72, 75, 87
context, xv, 7, 12, 14, 46, 63, 64, 66, 69–70, 77–78, 81, 116n8, 116n1
Covid-19, 6, 10, 27, 88, 99n8, 102n16, 103n28, 104n29, 111n19
credentials, 51, 78
Crenshaw, Kimberlé, 81, 119n14–15

deviance, 12, 14, 44–45, 48, 82, 107n57, 113n4
diversity, 37, 73, 76, 82, 84, 88, 117n3
divorce, 24, 35, 42, 64, 114n10
domestic load, 12, 25, 39, 45, 78, 96
empowerment, 14, 32, 50, 56–58, 72, 78, 79, 86, 87
encouragement, 17, 24, 30, 41, 45, 72
Enlightenment, 85
equilibrium, 12, 45, 98n5, 111n20, 115n17

faculty, 36, 39, 41, 53, 58, 59, 64, 65, 72, 73, 75, 88, 91
failure, 7, 11, 21, 50, 64, 69, 111n22
faith, 30, 40, 56, 63, 75, 78
family-affected decisions, 54
feminism, 23, 35, 36, 112n1
fertility rates, 11, 23
first woman, 4, 28, 29, 36, 59–60, 73, 78, 95
Fortune 500, 5

gender bias, 9, 14, 60
gender discrimination, xv, 4, 9–10, 14, 22, 75, 78, 81, 83, 87
gender revolution, 27, 98n5
gender roles, xiv, 1, 2, 14, 25, 40, 97n1
genderblind, 29, 74
glass ceiling, 3–5, 10, 14, 87
graduate school, xiii, 5, 33, 49, 51, 70, 95
greedy institution, 38–39, 69, 70, 78, 96
grit, 69, 76, 78

hegemonic imagination, 84–85
HERS institute, 46
hierarchy, 56–57, 91, 114n11
hiring, 27

ideal worker model, 38, 113n5, 113n7
imposter syndrome, 62, 116n7, 116n8

institutional type, 17, 34, 36, 48, 67, 68, 88, 109n74
anarchical, 34, 43, 48, 50–51, 68, 91, 94, 102n17, 115n2
bureaucratic, 34, 43, 48, 68, 70, 91, 93–94, 114n11
collegial, 34, 43, 48, 68, 91, 93, 114n11
political, 34, 43, 48, 50, 68, 73, 75, 91, 94, 115n2
interpersonal relationships, 37, 55
intersectionality, 81–82

labyrinth, 10, 14, 106n43
leadership development, 13, 33, 46
leadership style, 17, 55–57, 59, 62
life course. *See* sequencing
LGBTQ+, 75, 82, 97n1, 109n1
Locke, John, 85–86
loneliness/isolation, 6, 28, 30, 86–87
luck/fortune, 4, 17, 30, 66

maternal wall, 4, 10, 14, 87
mentorship/mentor, 17, 30–33, 45–47, 55, 60, 65–67, 72, 76, 87
coach, 13
encourager, 17, 30, 45
informal, 13, 30, 46
peer, 45, 66, 67
processor, 17, 30, 45, 65–67
sponsor. *See* sponsorship
meritocracy, 9, 22

Index

mindset, 14, 33, 112n28, 112n30
model/example, 8, 13, 14, 36, 38, 39, 57, 71, 76, 86, 87

NASA, 80
Neale Hurston, Zora, 83
networking, 14, 67, 71

oppression, 70, 84
opt-out revolution, 10, 12, 14, 101n15, 114n9

Parsons, Talcott, 85
passing (theory), 19–20, 109n1
pipeline, xv, 5, 13
pioneer. *See* first woman
policy, 4, 5, 7, 8, 9, 37
power, xiv, 1, 3, 5, 22, 58, 70, 79, 80, 82, 84–87, 98n3
pregnancy, 4, 102n20
professional development. *See* leadership development
purpose (sense of meaning), 49, 58, 79, 85, 87
The Pursuit of Happyness (movie), 20

Rand, Ayn, 89
religious, 1, 19, 91
responsiveness, 77–79, 82, 88, 117n5, 117n6
Roosevelt, Eleanor, 11

sampling/coding, 109n74
second shift, 7, 11, 14, 104n31

self-doubt, 30, 33, 34, 60–64, 68
self-efficacy, 24, 32
sequencing, 14, 16, 23, 26, 51–54, 110n11
single-axis analysis. *See* intersectionality
social construction, 20
social imagination, 83
social norms, 1, 8, 10, 12, 38, 43–45, 56, 59, 79, 86, 89, 96, 115n17
socialization, 14, 62
spiritual, 56
sponsorship, 13, 14, 17, 31–33, 38, 45, 51, 67, 87–88
    advocate, 13, 31, 32, 37, 51
    champion, 31, 32
    endorser, 31
sticky floor, 4, 10, 87
stigma, 20, 22, 109n5, 109n6
strategic, 27, 55, 67, 73, 78, 82
strength, 28, 42, 47, 55, 63, 68, 71, 76, 78, 85
supportive spouse, 24–27, 42, 60, 75

teamwork, 56–59
tenure, 42, 51, 52, 72, 73
Their Eyes Were Watching God (Neale Hurston), 83
third shift, 7
Tomlin, Lily, 11
Townes, Emilie, 84–85
trailing spouse, 26, 75

victim, 69, 79, 82, 116n2
viewpoint/perspective, 12, 21, 22, 24, 29, 37, 67, 87, 96

wage gap, 115n2
weak ties, 68, 116n10
weakness, 34, 61, 62

Weber, Max, 87
womanist studies, 81, 84
women's groups, 45–47
women's rights, 17, 35, 43, 48
work-life balance, xiii, 10, 36, 38, 53, 60, 95
World War II, 2, 101n12